THE NURSES GUIDE

TO STARTING

YOUR

OWN PRACTICE

VOLUME 1: FOR APRNS – OPENING AND RUNNING A PRIVATE PRACTICE

BY

Dr. Pauline Stoltzfus

PhD., MSN, APRN, FNP-BC, PMHNP-BC, CSAP

Dedication

This book is dedicated to Roy, Lilly, and Sophia.

To my husband Roy, thank you for believing in me, supporting every late night, every big idea, and every "what if." Your love and partnership make everything possible.

To my daughters, Lilly and Sophia, may you always know that you are strong, brilliant, and capable of building anything you dream. Watching you grow inspires me every day to be braver, bolder, and better. This book is for you, and because of you.

Part of a Groundbreaking Series for Healthcare Entrepreneurs

This is Volume 1 of a multi-part series designed to empower healthcare professionals at every level to build their own independent practice.

- **Volume 1** is written specifically for Advanced Practice Registered Nurses (APRNs) ready to open and operate their own clinics.
- **Volume 2** will be dedicated to Registered Nurses (RNs) looking to start concierge services, education-based businesses, IV hydration ventures, and more.
- **Volume 3** will focus on Medical Assistants (MAs) and Certified Nursing Assistants (CNAs) who want to build supportive, profitable service-based healthcare businesses in their own communities.

No matter where you are in your professional journey, this series will meet you there, with the tools, templates, and confidence to move forward.

TABLE OF CONTENTS

Introduction

Congratulations on taking the first step toward transforming your nursing career and owning your future. Whether you're reading this as an eBook on your couch or flipping through a printed copy between shifts, I'm proud of you for investing in yourself, and in your dream.

This book is your in-depth guide to starting and running your own private practice as a nurse practitioner. From choosing a business entity to credentialing with insurance companies, from leasing your first office to navigating billing, charting, and growth, you'll find everything you need in these pages. It's not just a blueprint; it's the playbook I wish I had when I started my own practice.

Nurse practitioners across the country are asking the same question: *How do I do this without going broke, getting burned out, or losing my passion for care?* This book is for you, the clinician who wants more autonomy, more purpose, and more alignment between your values and your work. You already have the clinical training. What you need now is the business knowledge to make your vision sustainable.

Inside, you'll find real-world examples, proven strategies, downloadable tools, and guidance on everything from selecting your electronic health recorder (EHR) and negotiating contracts to hiring staff and planning for the future. There are no fluff chapters here, just actionable advice rooted in experience.

I'm a dual-certified Family and Psychiatric Nurse Practitioner with a PhD in Educational Technology and Design. I built my first private practice from the ground up, while juggling motherhood, a shoestring budget, and a steep learning curve. I have built my business into the "Best of Northern Nevada" primary care practice. I know the hurdles, and I've turned them into stepping stones, so you don't have to learn the hard way.

This information has helped me launch and grow a profitable, mission-driven clinic in Northern Nevada. It's also helped other NPs avoid costly mistakes, streamline their operations, and gain the confidence to own their role as healthcare entrepreneurs.

So here's my ask: read this book actively. Take notes. Revisit chapters. Use the toolkit. And when fear or doubt creeps in, flip back to this introduction and remember why you started. Let's build something amazing, together.

PART I: Is Private Practice Right for You?

Welcome to the beginning of your journey. This section is all about self-reflection, clarity, and preparing your mindset and vision before diving into logistics. These chapters help you figure out if this path is right for you, and if it is, how to make sure you're building something intentional and sustainable from day one.

Chapter 1 We kick things off by exploring the bigger picture, why this is an ideal moment in history for nurse practitioners to go independent. From increasing patient demand to burnout in traditional settings, reimbursement parity, and the rise of telehealth, the timing is on your side.

Chapter 2 Now, it's time to look inward. Do you have what it takes to be both a clinician and a business owner? This chapter offers a candid checklist to assess your mindset, time, financial risk tolerance, and support system. It's not about being perfect, it's about being prepared. You'll walk away with a realistic picture of your personal readiness and the areas where you may need to grow.

Chapter 3 With clarity around your "why," we start to shape your "how." This chapter helps you define your target population, ideal services, mission, and values. You'll begin outlining what your practice will actually look like day to day, from the types of appointments you offer to the culture you want to build. It's the blueprint before the bricks.

Chapter 1: The NP Landscape, Why Now?

The healthcare landscape is undergoing a quiet revolution, and nurse practitioners (NPs) are at the center of it. As of 2025, more than half the states in the U.S. now grant full practice authority (FPA) to nurse practitioners, allowing them to evaluate patients, diagnose conditions, order and interpret diagnostic tests, and initiate and manage treatments, including prescribing medications, without physician oversight. This shift has fundamentally changed the opportunity landscape for NPs across the country.

The question is no longer "Can NPs own and run their own practices?" rather, "Why haven't more NPs done it already?" This chapter explores the unique moment in time we find ourselves in and why there has never been a better time to consider opening your own independent practice as a nurse practitioner.

The Shift Toward Full Practice Authority

A Brief History

Just two decades ago, the majority of NPs practiced under restricted or reduced authority. Most states required NPs to collaborate with or be supervised by physicians. Opening a solo NP-run practice was legally possible in some areas, but in practice, it was difficult and professionally stigmatized.

Fast forward to today: the COVID-19 pandemic, rising provider shortages, and increasing demand for accessible, affordable healthcare have created the perfect storm. States have reevaluated outdated regulatory frameworks, and the NP profession has stepped into the vacuum left by physician shortages, particularly in rural and underserved areas. As of 2025, 27 states plus Washington, D.C., offer full practice authority. Several states that previously required collaborative agreements have removed or relaxed them. National organizations such as the American Association of Nurse

Practitioners (AANP) continue to push for regulatory reform and recognition.

What Full Practice Authority Really Means

With full practice authority, nurse practitioners can operate independently without physician supervision, open and manage clinics, bill insurance directly, prescribe medications (including controlled substances with appropriate DEA licensure), and be listed as primary care providers. It also means that you, as an NP, can shape the entire patient experience, from intake to treatment to follow-up, in a way that reflects your values, training, and philosophy of care.

The Market Opportunity

A Nation Starving for Access

Despite technological advances, the U.S. healthcare system is buckling under its own weight. Patients are waiting longer than ever for primary care appointments, mental health services, and chronic disease management. According to the Association of American Medical Colleges, the U.S. could see a shortage of up to 124,000 physicians by 2034. This shortage is especially severe in rural areas, where entire counties may lack a single physician. Medicaid patients often struggle to find providers who accept them, and access to mental health care, particularly for adolescents and young adults, has reached crisis levels. Nurse practitioners are uniquely positioned to meet these needs. In many communities, NPs are already providing essential services. Opening your own practice gives you the freedom to meet these needs on your terms.

Niche Opportunities

Independent NPs aren't just filling gaps, they're building practices that reflect their passions and values. Many are opening family medicine practices with an integrative or functional medicine approach, while others are launching mental health clinics, substance use treatment centers, or wellness-based practices. Some are creating spaces specifically for underserved communities, like LGBTQIA+ health clinics or practices focused on adolescent care. The flexibility of independent practice means you can tailor your services, branding, and environment to the patients you want to serve most.

Technology and Tools That Level the Playing Field

Electronic Health Records (EHRs)
Modern EHR systems have made it easier than ever to run a streamlined, independent practice. Gone are the days of needing a large IT team to manage your records. Platforms like AthenaOne, Charm, Elation, and Jane are designed with smaller practices in mind. They are intuitive, affordable, and include features like telehealth integration, HIPAA-compliant messaging, automated billing, and even patient engagement tools.

Telehealth
Telehealth, once seen as a temporary solution during the pandemic, is now a standard part of healthcare delivery. With the right platform, you can reach rural patients, offer after-hours appointments, and build a flexible schedule that works for you and your patients. Some NPs are even operating entirely virtual practices, reducing overhead while maximizing reach.

Practice Management Software
Today's all-in-one practice management tools combine charting, scheduling, billing, and communication into one streamlined dashboard. Many of these platforms integrate with labs and pharmacies, further reducing administrative burden and allowing you to focus on patient care. They also make it easier to stay compliant with documentation and audit requirements.

Reimbursement
Reimbursement rates for nurse practitioners are rising, especially in states that grant full practice authority. Many insurers reimburse NPs at the same or nearly the same rate as physicians when serving as primary care providers. While credentialing can be a time-consuming process, it opens the door to insurance panels and sustainable long-term revenue.

Social and Professional Impact

Building Trust in Underserved Communities
Independent practices allow NPs to practice in alignment with the core nursing values of holistic, patient-centered care. This is especially important in underserved communities, where patients may have experienced discrimination or neglect in the traditional healthcare system. By taking

time, listening, and building rapport, NP-owned practices become trusted community anchors.

Professional Autonomy

Owning your own practice puts you in control of your time, clinical decisions, and workplace culture. You decide your hours. You choose which patients you want to see. You design your workflows and policies. And you set the tone for what healthcare should feel like, for both patients and staff. This kind of autonomy is not only professionally rewarding but also deeply empowering.

The Time Is Now

With full practice authority spreading, modern tools more accessible than ever, and the need for compassionate, comprehensive care only growing, this is a turning point for nurse practitioners. If you've been waiting for permission, this is it. If you've been wondering whether you're qualified, you are. The chapters ahead will walk you through every step of this journey, from refining your vision to launching your business and scaling it sustainably. You already have the clinical knowledge. Now it's time to build the business around it.

Chapter 2: Entrepreneurial Readiness – Are You Built for This?

Becoming an entrepreneur isn't just a business decision, it's a mindset shift. Most nurse practitioners have spent their careers working in structured environments, where clinical protocols, schedules, and support systems are already in place. Owning a practice flips that model on its head. You won't just be providing care, you'll be leading a team, managing operations, setting a vision, and navigating the many moving parts of a small business. This chapter is designed to help you take an honest inventory of your readiness, emotionally, financially, and professionally, to take on the role of a business owner.

The Emotional Reality of Business Ownership

Launching a private practice is exhilarating, but it's not without stress. There will be late nights, self-doubt, and decisions that don't have clear right answers. You'll face the weight of financial risk and the discomfort of growing pains. Are you willing to step outside your comfort zone and sit with uncertainty? Can you continue to lead even when you feel unsure?

If you still feel the need to have someone constantly checking your work, signing off on decisions, or validating your every move, you may not be ready for practice ownership, yet. Being your own boss means the buck stops with you, clinically and operationally. You need to be confident in your skills, your judgment, and your medical knowledge.

What gets most successful NP entrepreneurs through these hurdles isn't perfection, it's resilience. The ability to bounce back from setbacks, learn from mistakes, and keep showing up is more important than any business degree. If you've ever juggled a full patient load, comforted a dying patient, or held your ground during a code, you already know what it means to show up under pressure. Those same skills translate directly to leadership.

Shifting from Clinician to CEO

Many NPs struggle in the transition from clinical expert to practice leader. You're used to being the go-to person for patient care; however, running a business requires you to develop entirely new competencies. You'll be expected to manage people, handle financial decisions, make strategic plans, and market your services effectively. Each of these areas requires a different part of your brain and a willingness to grow beyond your comfort zone.

That said, you don't need to be an expert in everything. There are resources, mentors, consultants, and courses to help guide you. What matters most is having the humility to admit what you don't know and the curiosity to go find out. Entrepreneurship is a continual learning process, and what you lack in business knowledge today, you can build as you go.

Time Management and Boundaries

When you run a practice, everything competes for your attention. Between patients, staff, phone calls, paperwork, credentialing, and marketing, it can feel like a never-ending list. That's why successful practice owners are relentless about protecting their time. Ask yourself whether you're comfortable delegating tasks or if you tend to take everything on yourself. Can you set boundaries with patients, vendors, and even friends when needed? Do you understand your own limits and energy rhythms?

Building a sustainable practice means knowing when to say yes, and when to say no. It means setting realistic expectations, creating structure, and being intentional with your time. No matter how passionate you are, burnout is a real risk. Clear boundaries are not just helpful, they're essential. Make sure you can truly ask yourself, "is this a good use of MY time?" If the answer is no, and someone else can do whatever task, delegate it.

Financial Readiness

Starting a practice is an investment. You'll need startup capital, a cushion for the early months when revenue is low, and a plan for managing ongoing expenses. While I'll go deeper into costs in later chapters, now is the time to assess your personal financial health. Ask yourself, "do I have debt that could limit my access to financing?" "How's my credit score?" "Am I prepared to cover personal expenses if my income fluctuates?" "Have I created a savings buffer?" You don't need to be wealthy to start a practice, but you do need to be realistic. Many NPs start small: they sublease an office, offer telehealth part-time, or maintain per diem work while building their patient panel. If you're resourceful and prepared to plan carefully, there are creative ways to reduce financial risk.

Support Systems Matter

No one builds a successful practice alone. From day one, you'll need support, both professionally and personally. Do you have people in your life who believe in your vision? Are you willing to invest in professional relationships that can guide you through this process?

That support might come from a mentor who has opened a practice before, (thank you, Cameron), a CPA or bookkeeper who understands healthcare finance, or a healthcare attorney who can review your contracts. It might also come from a close friend (thank you, Andy) or partner who can offer encouragement and perspective when things get tough. Community is one of the greatest assets a nurse practitioner can cultivate. Find your people early, and don't be afraid to ask for help.

Imposter Syndrome and Self-Doubt

Nearly every NP who has opened a practice has faced the fear of "not being ready." You may wonder if you're too young, too inexperienced, or too behind. Here's the truth: no one feels 100% ready. And waiting for that perfect moment often leads to never starting at all.

You are more prepared than you think. You've earned advanced degrees. You've cared for complex patients. You've navigated systems that weren't built for you and made them work anyway. This is the same grit and adaptability that will carry you through entrepreneurship. If you feel fear, you're normal. If you feel called, if the idea of building something of your own won't leave you alone, then you owe it to yourself to explore it.

Final Reflection: Are You Ready to Lead?

Take a moment to reflect. Not on whether you know every answer, rather on whether you're willing to find them. Not on whether it will be hard, but on whether it will be worth it. The nurse practitioner model of care is grounded in presence, critical thinking, and compassion. These same traits are what make NPs excellent business owners. This chapter isn't here to scare you, it's here to prepare you. To ask the right questions before you dive in. If your answer is yes, or even "maybe, and I'm curious", then you're already on your way. Let's keep building.

Chapter 3: Laying the Foundation – Planning Your Practice

Before a patient ever walks through your door or logs into your telehealth portal, you need to build the infrastructure that will support your private practice, and that starts with planning. This chapter will walk you through how to clarify your vision, choose your initial service offerings, and determine whether your plan is viable both financially and logistically. It's not just about dreaming big, it's about making smart, informed decisions that will carry you through the early months and beyond.

Defining Your Vision

Every successful business starts with a clear vision. Why do you want to open a practice? What kind of care do you want to deliver, and to whom? Your answers to these questions will shape everything from your branding and marketing strategy to your services and staffing. Maybe you're driven by a desire to offer high-quality primary care in an area with limited access. Or perhaps you're passionate about mental health and want to integrate behavioral services into a family practice setting. Starting broad gives you flexibility while you grow your patient base and learn where your time and effort are most needed.

As your practice evolves, your vision may sharpen. Many NPs start with general services and naturally gravitate toward a specific population or type of care based on what their community needs and what they personally enjoy. This organic narrowing of focus is often more sustainable than starting out too narrowly defined.

Starting Broad, Then Refining

While niche practices may seem appealing, especially from a marketing standpoint, they can be hard to build from scratch. Unless you're in a highly populated area with substantial demand, starting out too specific can limit your growth. Most NPs find success by offering general services, family medicine, wellness exams, basic chronic disease management, mental health evaluations, and gradually identifying patterns within their patient population.

Over time, you might discover that 60% of your patients come to you for weight management. Or that you're consistently seeing high demand for adolescent mental health support. That's when you start to narrow your messaging, tailor services, and possibly rebrand to reflect a more focused identity. This approach allows you to scale based on real data, not just aspiration.

Understanding Market Demand

Once you've defined your general scope, the next step is understanding if your idea is viable in your area, or through telehealth. This is where market research comes in. What other providers are operating in your region? Are there service gaps you could fill? Is your target population geographically or virtually accessible?

Start by searching online to see how many clinics are offering similar services. Look at insurance directories, Google Maps, and community health reports. Check in with your state board, Medicaid program, or HRSA to identify areas with provider shortages. If you're planning to operate online, ask yourself where your licensure allows you to practice. Are you authorized in states with high demand for your services? Does the demographic you want to serve use telehealth comfortably? Realistic planning starts with real data.

Business Planning: Making It Real

At this stage, it's time to put everything together in a formal business plan. This isn't just for lenders, it's for you. A well-written business plan outlines your mission, services, market strategy, competitive analysis, financial projections, and growth plan. It clarifies your next steps and gives you a professional roadmap to follow. Even if no one else reads it, you'll benefit from putting your ideas on paper. It forces you to think critically, adjust your expectations, and identify gaps before they become roadblocks. It's okay if it evolves over time; that's part of the process.

Final Thoughts

Starting a practice without a plan is like driving cross-country without a map. You might still get there, but not without unnecessary stress, backtracking, and wrong turns. When you take time now to clarify your vision, understand your market, and build a financial foundation, you're not just launching a business; you're building something sustainable and impactful.

Planning isn't the exciting part. It's not what you'll post about on social media or celebrate with a ribbon cutting; it's what sets the stage for all of those moments to come. And you're already doing it, right now. Next, we'll take this vision and begin building the legal and structural components that turn your dream into a real, operating practice.

PART II: Planning Your Practice

Welcome to the part of the journey where your private practice stops being just an idea and starts becoming real. In this section, we focus on the foundational steps that bring your vision to life, legally, structurally, financially, and strategically. These chapters aren't about fluff; they're about doing the real work of setting up a sustainable, compliant, and fundable practice.

Chapter 4 starts with the absolute essentials: registering your business, getting your EIN, choosing a business structure (LLC, S-Corp, or PC), opening a bank account, and setting up systems for bookkeeping and budgeting. These are the backend decisions that will determine whether your practice runs smoothly or becomes a logistical mess. We also get into insurance, malpractice, liability, and everything else you'll need to protect your business before your first patient walks in the door.

Chapter 5 dives into credentialing, often the most tedious but absolutely a critical step in getting paid. I'll walk you through obtaining your NPI-1 and NPI-2, creating your CAQH profile, and applying to Medicare, Medicaid, and commercial insurance panels. You'll learn why a clean fax number setup matters, how to write a simple and effective letter of intent, and how to avoid common delays that could cost you months of revenue.

Chapter 6 covers funding your dream. We explore bootstrapping, SBA and traditional loans, and grant opportunities from HRSA and local programs. You'll also learn what lenders and funders are really looking for, and how to make your case with confidence. This chapter is about giving yourself permission to ask for support and equipping you with the plan that makes it possible.

Chapter 7 pulls it all together into a business plan that doesn't just sit on a shelf. Whether you're applying for funding or just need a roadmap, you need to articulate your mission, define your services, analyze your market, build realistic revenue projections, and map out your growth. You'll even get examples and editable templates to make the process easier.

This section is where your practice gets its legs. It's detailed, yes, but it's also empowering. Once you've built a solid plan and foundation, you're no longer just dreaming about opening your own practice; you're actually doing it.

Chapter Four: Business Licenses, Entity Types, and Insurance

Once you've developed your vision and a realistic plan, the next step is giving your practice a legal identity. This part might not feel as exciting as designing your logo or choosing your EHR, but it's foundational. Getting the structure right at the start protects you legally, makes financial management easier, and helps you avoid costly missteps down the road. This chapter will walk you through choosing a business structure, registering your business, obtaining licenses, and preparing for compliance in the ever-evolving world of private healthcare.

Choosing the Right Business Entity

Your first legal decision is how to structure your business. The most common options for nurse practitioners include a sole proprietorship, a limited liability company (LLC), a professional corporation (PC), or an S-corporation. Each has pros and cons related to taxes, liability, and paperwork.

For many NPs, an LLC is the most straightforward and protective option. It separates your personal assets from your business, provides flexibility in how you're taxed, and is relatively simple to maintain. Some states require healthcare businesses to form a Professional LLC (PLLC) or Professional Corporation (PC), so it's important to check your state's rules.

Choosing an S-Corp status can sometimes save money on taxes by allowing you to pay yourself a reasonable salary and take the rest as distributions, which are not subject to self-employment tax. However, this structure comes with stricter IRS requirements and more complex bookkeeping. It's worth speaking to a CPA or healthcare attorney before making a final decision. Getting this step right the first time saves time and hassle later.

Registering Your Business

Once you choose your structure, you'll need to register your business name with the Secretary of State or relevant business authority in your state. This process typically involves a small fee and can often be completed online. You'll also need to register for an Employer Identification Number (EIN) with the IRS. This is your business's version of a Social Security number and is required for tax filing, payroll, and opening a business bank account.

If you're planning to operate under a name other than your own or your LLC name, you'll likely need to file a DBA (Doing Business As) with your county or state. In addition, open a dedicated business checking account to separate your finances. This helps with taxes, audits, and bookkeeping, and is a step toward building business credit for future growth.

Licensing and Credentialing Essentials

You'll need several licenses and registrations to operate legally. At a minimum, this includes your valid NP license in your practicing state and DEA registration for prescribing controlled substances. Many states also require a state-level controlled substance license in addition to your federal DEA number. You'll also need malpractice insurance appropriate for your specialty and scope of practice, along with business licenses or permits as required by your city, county, or state.

Another essential early step is applying for a National Provider Identifier (NPI). This 10-digit identification number is issued by the Centers for Medicare and Medicaid Services (CMS) and is required for billing insurance, writing prescriptions, and identifying you as a healthcare provider. You'll need both an individual NPI (Type 1) and, if you are opening your own business, an organizational NPI (Type 2).

Credentialing with insurance companies and Medicare/Medicaid is its own separate, often frustrating process. You'll complete extensive applications, provide supporting documentation, and follow up regularly. Most insurers require you to use CAQH, a universal credentialing system. You'll need to create and maintain a profile there with up-to-date information, including your NPI, licenses, malpractice coverage, and more.

Because credentialing can take several months, it's wise to begin the process early, long before you see your first patient. Being proactive helps ensure you can begin billing insurance from day one.

Compliance and Legal Protections

Healthcare is one of the most regulated industries in the country, and protecting your practice requires early and ongoing attention to compliance. HIPAA compliance is essential, particularly if you're managing patient records electronically. Be sure to select an EHR with built-in security features and train yourself and your staff on maintaining privacy and data protection.

If you have a physical location, OSHA regulations apply as well. You'll need to ensure safe working conditions, manage sharps disposal, and prepare for emergencies. Employment law is another area that requires care. Know the difference between hiring a W2 employee and a 1099 contractor, as misclassifying staff can result in penalties.

Telehealth adds another layer of complexity. Each state has its own regulations regarding consent, documentation, and licensure. If you plan to see patients across state lines, make sure your licensure and platform are compliant with local rules.

Having written policies in place for HIPAA, OSHA, employment, and telehealth, even if you're the only employee, can help protect you legally and demonstrate good faith in the event of a dispute or audit.

Insurance and Risk Management

In addition to malpractice insurance, consider other types of insurance to safeguard your business. General liability insurance covers non-clinical incidents like a patient slipping in your office. If you're operating a physical clinic, it's essential. If you employ staff, you'll likely need workers' compensation insurance, and if you have employees working in other states, such as for telehealth, you will need workers' compensation insurance for the state they reside. Employment practices liability insurance (EPLI) can help protect you in the event of hiring disputes or workplace claims. Even if you're confident in your systems, insurance is your safety net. Think of it as your practice's seatbelt; you hope you won't need it, but you'll be glad it's there if you do.

Final Thoughts

Legal and structural planning may not be glamorous, except it's a core part of launching a solid and successful practice. Skipping these steps or cutting corners can cost you dearly later on. With the right foundation, you'll be positioned to grow with confidence, knowing your practice is not just clinically excellent, it's legally sound. In the next chapter, we'll begin Section 2: Building Your Foundation, starting with how to choose your niche and connect with your ideal patient base.

Chapter 5: Credentialing with Insurance – Getting Paid Starts Here

Credentialing is the bridge between your practice and the financial sustainability it needs to survive. Without it, you can't bill insurance, Medicaid, Medicare, or commercial plans, and without billing, you're working for free. It's a time-consuming process that demands organization, persistence, and precision. If you simply start early and plan wisely, you'll set yourself up for smoother reimbursement and fewer headaches later.

In this chapter, we'll walk through exactly how to get credentialed, starting with the basics like your National Provider Identifier (NPI) and CAQH profile, and then moving into the complex web of payers, including Medicare Fee-for-Service (FFS), Medicaid, managed care organizations (MCOs), and commercial plans. You'll also get practical tips drawn from real-world lessons, like why your fax number matters more than you think.

Start with the Basics: NPI, EIN, and Business License

As soon as you register your business and obtain an Employer Identification Number (EIN) from the IRS, you should begin preparing for credentialing. Your business license, National Provider Identifier (NPI) and EIN are required by nearly every payer.

There are two types of NPIs:

NPI-1 is your personal identifier as a provider.

NPI-2 is for your organization or business entity.

You can apply for both through the National Plan and Provider Enumeration System (NPPES) at https://nppes.cms.hhs.gov. These numbers are used across all insurance panels, so getting them early and making sure they match across systems is essential.

CAQH: Your Credentialing Hub

The Council for Affordable Quality Healthcare (CAQH) is a centralized database that nearly all commercial insurance companies use to credential providers. Once you've secured your NPI and EIN, go to https://proview.caqh.org and create a profile. You'll be asked to upload a significant amount of information including:

Board certifications, professional licenses, malpractice insurance, work history, practice location(s), tax ID, legal business name, and more. Be thorough and double-check for accuracy. Any discrepancies can delay the process. You'll also want to keep this profile up to date every time anything changes, new address, new phone number, or updated insurance documents. Many systems check your CAQH profile automatically during recredentialing.

The Letter of Intent

Many payers require a letter of intent when you request to join their network. This should include all of the core information about your practice:

- Name of your group or practice
- Provider name and credentials
- Specialty and board certifications
- Tax ID (EIN) and both NPIs
- Physical and mailing addresses
- Phone and fax numbers
- Email address
- CAQH ID number
- Hospital affiliations (if any)

This letter signals your intention to enroll and gives the payer what they need to begin the process. Having a clean, professional letter ready to go saves time and presents you as an organized, credible applicant. The letter of intent can be simple bullet points as well, don't go crazy with it, just give the information in a clear, concise manner.

Practical Tip: Choose a Convertible Fax Number

Here's a lesson learned the hard way, when setting up your phone and fax lines, choose numbers that are portable across platforms. Initially, I used an e-fax that emailed all faxes to my email inbox. It worked fine at first, but when I chose an EHR that required fax integration, I learned that my number couldn't be ported into their system. Changing it meant updating that number with every insurance company I had already credentialed with, which became a nightmare. Avoid this by selecting a fax number from a provider that can be transferred later, such as your local phone company or a major VoIP service.

Understanding Insurance Types and Reimbursements

Before you begin credentialing, it's essential to understand the different types of insurance plans you'll be working with. Each has its own rules, reimbursement methods, and patient cost-sharing structures.

Medicare is a federal program primarily for individuals aged 65 and older, though younger people may qualify if they have certain disabilities or end-stage renal disease. Providers apply for Medicare enrollment through the PECOS system at https://pecos.cms.hhs.gov.

Traditional Medicare includes:

Part A: Hospital coverage

Part B: Outpatient medical services

Part D: Prescription coverage (optional, separate cost for the patient)

Original Medicare typically pays 80% of the approved rate for covered services, with the patient responsible for the remaining 20%. It does *not* include dental, vision, or hearing unless a patient purchases separate Part D or supplemental coverage.

Medicare Advantage Plans (Part C) Medicare Advantage Plans are offered by private insurers but must follow federal Medicare guidelines. These plans typically bundle Parts A, B, and sometimes D, and operate more like commercial plans. Rather than the 80/20 split, these plans often have structured copays, deductibles, and out-of-pocket maximums.

Patients on Medicare Advantage may owe a flat copay per visit or a percentage of the cost, depending on their plan. These structures vary widely and can feel more familiar to those used to commercial insurance.

Medicaid is a state-administered, federally supported program for low-income individuals and families. Application processes and eligibility criteria vary by state. Many states contract with Managed Care Organizations (MCOs) to deliver Medicaid services.

Some patients are "dual eligible," meaning they have Medicare as their primary insurance and Medicaid as secondary. In these cases, Medicaid often covers what Medicare doesn't, such as the remaining 20%, prescriptions, or services Medicare excludes.

> ***Pro Tip:*** Be aware that Medicaid typically does not allow charging patients any out-of-pocket fees for covered services, including no-show fees or charges for completing forms.

Commercial Insurance Commercial insurance includes health plans purchased through employers, unions, or directly by individuals through the healthcare marketplace. Major payers include Blue Cross Blue Shield, Aetna, Cigna, UnitedHealthcare, and several other providers. Most people under age 65 who don't qualify for Medicare or Medicaid fall into this category.

These plans vary widely, not just from one insurer to another, but even between subplans offered by the same company. For example, two patients with "Blue Cross" cards may have completely different benefits, copay structures, deductibles, and covered services.

Most commercial plans fall into one of the following structures:

- *Fixed Copay Plans*: Patients pay a flat amount per visit ($25 for primary care, $50 for specialists, etc.), and the insurer pays the rest.

- *Coinsurance Plans*: Patients pay a percentage (20%, 30%, etc.) of the visit cost until they reach their out-of-pocket maximum.

- *High-Deductible Health Plans (HDHPs)*: Patients must meet a large deductible before the insurance pays anything.

With high-deductible plans, you'll still bill the patient's insurance. The payer then sends you an Explanation of Benefits (EOB) that shows how much the patient owes, based on your contracted rate, which is often significantly higher than your cash pay rate. This can lead to patient frustration when they realize they owe more through their insurance than they would have if they'd paid out of pocket. However, you are legally and contractually obligated to collect the full contracted rate, even if it seems unfair to the patient.

Your reimbursement rate with commercial payers is part of your credentialing contract. When you apply to be in-network with a payer, they issue you a fee schedule that outlines how much they'll pay for each CPT code. You can and should review these rates and negotiate if they're below market or unsustainable for your practice. Many NPs don't realize they have this right, or assume they have no leverage. In truth, payers often expect negotiation, and even a modest increase can make a big difference in long-term revenue. You can request a rate increase at recredentialing time or periodically based on volume, inflation, or regional benchmarks. A sample letter requesting higher reimbursement is included later in this book to guide you through that process.

Commercial insurance plans typically include prescription drug coverage, but the specifics also vary dramatically. Formularies (approved medication lists) are updated frequently, and patients may require prior authorizations, step therapy, or appeals to obtain coverage for their medications. Your staff will likely spend a significant amount of time coordinating medication access.

Because of this complexity, it's important to:
- Verify benefits prior to visits.
- Clearly communicate patient financial responsibility.
- Create transparent office policies.
- Train front desk staff to walk patients through their plan details when needed.

Navigating commercial insurance is a challenge, but it's one you can master with preparation and confidence. Strategic credentialing, clear policies, and consistent patient communication are your best tools.

PPO vs HMO vs EPO – Why It Matters

It's not enough to be credentialed, you also need to understand how different plan types impact billing, reimbursement, and administrative workflow. These differences affect everything from whether you get paid to what paperwork is required at the front desk.

PPOs (Preferred Provider Organizations) offer patients more flexibility. They can see out-of-network providers at a higher cost and usually don't need referrals to specialists. As a provider, once you're credentialed and in-network, claims are generally processed without much administrative friction.

HMOs (Health Maintenance Organizations) are more restrictive. Patients must select a primary care provider (PCP) who acts as a gatekeeper for all care. If you're a family or primary care practice, make sure you are listed as the patient's designated PCP on file. If you're not listed on their plan/card, you won't get paid, even if you're credentialed with that plan. If you're a specialist, you'll typically need a referral from the patient's PCP before delivering services, or you won't get paid.

POS (Point of Service) plans are a hybrid between PPO and HMO structures. Like HMOs, they require referrals from a PCP (and again, you must be that listed PCP to be recognized). However, POS plans allow patients to go out-of-network, though at a higher cost to the patient. This flexibility makes them a bit more forgiving, but still administratively heavy.

EPOs (Exclusive Provider Organizations) EPOs also blend elements of PPOs and HMOs. Patients must use in-network providers, and out-of-network care is generally not covered, except in true emergencies. Referral requirements vary by plan; some EPOs require specialist referrals, others do not. From a provider standpoint, it's essential to verify these nuances in advance.

Understanding these distinctions enables you to effectively train your front desk staff to verify eligibility and referral requirements, and check if you're listed as the PCP (when applicable). It also helps ensure you submit clean claims, the kind that get paid the first time and don't bounce back due to something as small as a missing designation or unchecked box.

Pro Tip: *Watch for Select Networks & Underwritten Plans*

Be cautious of EPOs, "Select Networks," or plans "underwritten by" other carriers. Just because you're credentialed with Blue Cross doesn't mean you're in-network for all plans that carry the Blue Cross label. If a plan is underwritten by a third-party and you're not credentialed with that third-party, then you're considered out-of-network, even if the patient's card says Blue Cross. This is a common and frustrating credentialing trap, so double-check every time.

Medicare Comes First

If you want to be in-network with Medicare Advantage plans or many commercial carriers, you must first be credentialed with traditional Medicare Fee-for-Service (FFS). This is the original Medicare program managed by the federal government, and it's a prerequisite for many other plans.

You'll apply through the PECOS system. This is Medicare's online portal for provider enrollment: https://pecos.cms.hhs.gov. Be prepared for a detailed application, and have all your documents ready, including your NPI, license, malpractice coverage, and business documents. Approval can take several weeks to several months, depending on your location. Once you're credentialed with Medicare FFS, you will receive your Medicare Provider Number, and only then will many commercial plans consider you eligible to apply to their networks.

Medicaid and MCOs

Medicaid programs vary by state, and most include a combination of traditional state Medicaid and managed care organizations (MCOs). First, apply directly with your state's Medicaid program. Medicaid may be called something different in your state, such as Medi-Cal (CA), TennCare (TN), or Apple Health (WA), among others. Search your state's official Medicaid portal to ensure accurate enrollment. It's best to search "[Your State] Medicaid Provider Enrollment" for the official application site. In many states, you must be enrolled in the Medicaid Fee-for-Service program before you can join any MCO panels. Once accepted, you'll typically receive a Medicaid provider ID number. This number will then be used to apply to each MCO operating in your state. Examples include plans run by Aetna, Anthem, Molina, or UnitedHealthcare Community Plan.

> *Pro Tip:* Apply for Medicaid enrollment twice, once using your NPI-1 (individual) and once with your NPI-2 (group or business entity). Some MCOs credential and reimburse under the individual provider, while others use the group entity. If you're not credentialed

under both through Medicaid FFS, you may get stuck midway through an MCO application when they can't locate the appropriate record. Save yourself time by enrolling both up front.

Commercial Insurance Panels

Commercial insurers include household names like Aetna, Blue Cross Blue Shield, Cigna, and UnitedHealthcare. Some of these plans may allow NPs to credential as independent providers, while others may require you to be part of a group or have a collaborative agreement, depending on state laws and payer policy.

Each company has its own process, and most will ask for the same core documents: CAQH profile, NPIs, license, malpractice insurance, business license, and tax ID. The timeline varies; many take 60 to 120 days to complete credentialing.

> ***Pro Tip:*** Apply to all of them at once as soon as your basic documents are ready. Don't wait until your Medicare or Medicaid credentialing is done to start commercial applications. If you have your EIN, NPI, business license, and CAQH ready, you can begin immediately. The insurance companies just may not finalize the contract until you have your Medicare or Medicaid number, but it's much easier to give it to them at the end than wait months to start the application process.

Final Thoughts

Credentialing is tedious, but absolutely essential. The sooner you start, the better. Don't try to piece it together as you go. Get your documents in order, organize them in a shared folder or system, and stay proactive with follow-up. Each payer is different, but all want the same thing: proof that you are licensed, insured, and legitimate. If you show them that from the start, your path to reimbursement will be much smoother. In the next chapter, we'll explore business structures like LLCs, S-Corps, and Professional Corporations, so you can decide which foundation makes the most sense for your practice.

Chapter 6: Funding Your Dream

Every great business begins with a bold idea; however, it takes money to make it a reality. Whether you're furnishing an office, investing in software, or floating your payroll until the revenue flows, startup capital is essential. Fortunately, you don't need to have it all in your bank account on day one. There are multiple paths to funding your private practice, each with its own advantages and trade-offs. In this chapter, we'll explore bootstrapping, loans, grants, and what financial institutions actually look for when evaluating healthcare startups. We'll also discuss opportunities through HRSA and local business incubators that many nurse practitioners overlook.

Bootstrapping: Starting Small with Your Own Funds

Bootstrapping means funding your business using personal savings, part-time income, or reinvesting early revenue. Many nurse practitioners start this way, especially those launching part-time or telehealth-only practices. The advantage of bootstrapping is that it allows you full control with no debt or external obligations. You set the pace.

However, this method can be slow. If your savings are limited, you'll need to make lean decisions, minimal staff, home office setups, and DIY marketing. It's a solid route if you're risk-averse or want to test the waters before fully committing. Just be sure to create a cash flow plan so you don't overextend yourself personally.

Loans: Borrowing to Build

If your startup needs exceed what you can self-fund, a small business loan can help you build faster. The most common options include:

- **SBA Loans:** The U.S. Small Business Administration guarantees loans from approved lenders, which reduces risk and opens access to better terms. These loans are ideal for larger capital needs like full build-outs or equipment purchases.
- **Traditional Bank Loans:** If you have a strong credit score and collateral, many banks will fund healthcare businesses, especially

if you've already registered your business, completed a budget, and have revenue projections.

- **Business Lines of Credit:** These offer flexibility. You're approved for a set amount, and you only pay interest on what you actually use. This is a great option for covering uneven cash flow or unexpected costs.

Lenders will often request your business plan, startup budget, personal credit score, proof of licensure, and projected revenue. Having these documents polished and ready shows that you're prepared and serious.

Grants: Free Money (with Strings Attached)

Grants don't need to be repaid, making them an attractive option, especially for practices that serve underserved communities or align with public health goals; although, they come with strings: extensive applications, reporting requirements, and strict usage guidelines. The Health Resources and Services Administration (HRSA) offers grants and loan repayment programs for providers in designated shortage areas. If you're opening in a Health Professional Shortage Area (HPSA) or plan to serve Medicaid/uninsured populations, you may be eligible. You can find HRSA opportunities at https://bhw.hrsa.gov/funding.

Also, explore your state's Office of Rural Health, local nonprofit hospitals, and public health departments, which often offer startup funds or mini-grants for behavioral health, substance use treatment, maternal care, or chronic disease management.

Local Business Incubators and Community Resources

Many communities offer more support than you might expect. Look for:

- **Small Business Development Centers (SBDCs):** These centers offer free advising, business plan support, and sometimes even access to microloans.
- **Women's Business Centers and Minority Business Development Agencies:** These organizations often help nurse practitioners navigate funding and certification opportunities.
- **Local credit unions and banks:** Some offer lower-barrier loans or mentorship programs specifically for healthcare startups.

- **Healthcare incubators or coworking spaces:** These might offer shared medical space with reduced rent for new practitioners.

What Lenders and Grant Committees Want to See

Whether you're seeking a loan or applying for a grant, funders want to see more than passion, they want a viable plan. You'll need:

- A clear mission and description of your services
- Market research or data showing demand
- Startup and operational budgets
- Projected revenue and expenses for at least 12–24 months
- Your licensure, certifications, and experience
- Any partnerships or affiliations that strengthen your plan
- How you will generate continued financial sustainability

Be honest about your needs, and also about how you plan to achieve sustainability. The more detailed and data-backed your projections are, the more fundable you'll appear.

Final Thoughts

Funding your dream doesn't have to mean going into massive debt or waiting until you have every dollar in hand. There are many routes to capital, and many nurse practitioners mix and match: bootstrapping for flexibility, grants for specific services, and a line of credit for safety. No matter which route you choose, be prepared, be organized, and don't be afraid to advocate for yourself. Your practice will serve your community, and that mission deserves investment. Next up, we'll help you write a business plan that goes beyond fluff and actually becomes your playbook.

Chapter 7: Writing a Business Plan That Actually Gets Used

Let's be honest, most business plans are written once, filed away, and never looked at again. Yet, yours shouldn't be. A well-written business plan is more than just a funding tool; it's your personal blueprint. It helps you make decisions, stay focused, evaluate opportunities, and track progress. If done right, it becomes the guide you return to again and again.

This chapter walks you through the core components of a real-world business plan: your mission and vision, service offerings, market analysis, revenue projections, SWOT breakdown, and marketing strategy. Since I know you're not starting a Fortune 500 company, I'll keep it practical and focused on what actually matters for nurse practitioner-owned practices.

Mission, Vision, and Services

Start with your "why." Your mission should describe what your practice exists to do, whether that's improving access to behavioral health, offering whole-person family care, or delivering trauma-informed services to underserved communities. It should be succinct and values-driven. Your vision goes a step further. It's your big-picture aspiration. What will your practice look like in five or ten years? What kind of legacy do you want to leave? Next, outline your core services. Will you provide primary care? Psychiatric medication management? IV hydration? Men's health? Be clear and specific. This helps you focus, and it helps funders and partners understand your niche.

Market Analysis

This is where you explain why your practice is needed. Include local demographic data, provider shortage maps, or statistics about access to care in your area. Is your region a Health Professional Shortage Area (HPSA)? Are there long waitlists for certain specialties? Are there large Medicaid or uninsured populations with limited access? If you're targeting a specific niche, say postpartum mental health or gender-affirming care, describe that population. What are their barriers to care? Who is (or isn't) serving them now? Real data here builds credibility and shows you've done your homework.

Revenue Projections

This is where many clinicians get nervous, except, it doesn't have to be complicated. A helpful starting point is checking current reimbursement rates. Medicare's Physician Fee Schedule can give you a baseline for common CPT codes, especially the evaluation and management codes (99202–99205 for new patients and 99212–99215 for established patients), as well as procedural codes relevant to your specialty. You can search fees by location, modifier, and service. https://www.cms.gov/medicare/physician-fee-schedule/search.

Some states have implemented Medicaid pay parity, reimbursing nurse practitioners at the same rate as physicians, and a growing number of commercial insurance companies have adopted similar policies. Be sure to research your state's Medicaid policies and commercial payer guidelines, as this can significantly affect your projected revenue and long-term sustainability.

Start by projecting how many patients you expect to see weekly, how much you'll charge (or receive from payers), and how that translates into monthly revenue. Factor in payer mix, Medicaid, Medicare, commercial, and cash, and be realistic about reimbursement rates. Then list your fixed and variable expenses and calculate when you expect to break even. Projections should cover at least the first 12 months, with a basic 3-year outlook if you're seeking funding. You don't have to predict the future perfectly. What matters is that you've thought it through.

SWOT: Strengths, Weaknesses, Opportunities, Threats

This simple tool helps you think strategically. What are your strengths (such as dual certification, community ties, etc.)? What gaps or weaknesses might hold you back (such as no staff yet, limited marketing experience, etc.)? Where are your growth opportunities? Perhaps there's a local employer looking for occupational health services or a regional shortage in addiction medicine. What external threats do you need to monitor: policy changes, new competition, or reimbursement shifts? A SWOT analysis makes your plan honest and actionable. It helps you build on what's working and prepare for what's not.

Marketing Plan

You don't need a marketing degree to promote your practice; you need a strategy. Start with your brand: What makes you different, and how will people find you? Will you focus on word of mouth, a strong Google Business profile, social media, or referral partnerships? Think about where your ideal patients spend time and how they search for care.

Your plan should include:

- A basic website with services, location, and how to book
- Google My Business and SEO for local search visibility
- Online reviews and testimonials
- Partnerships with therapists, school counselors, or primary care providers, if you're a specialist

Don't forget to budget time and money for marketing. Even the best services won't help people if they don't know you exist.

Real-World Templates and Examples

You don't have to start from scratch. At the end of this book, you'll find editable business plan templates tailored to nurse practitioner practices, along with real examples (with names changed) from startup clinics around the country. Use these as a jumping-off point, not a rigid mold. Your plan should reflect your community, your services, and your voice.

Final Thoughts

Writing a business plan is a lot like writing a care plan: it helps you understand the situation, identify goals, and develop a path to success. It shouldn't be static. Revisit it regularly, especially when you're making big decisions, applying for funding, or evaluating your progress. Coming up next, I'll walk through the logistics of where and how to open your doors, from negotiating leases to setting up your first office.

PART III: Building the Infrastructure

This is where your vision starts to take shape beyond paper. You've planned your services and structured your business; now it's time to build the physical and operational foundation that makes your practice functional, compliant, and patient-ready. In this section, we tackle the nuts and bolts of running a clinic, from your office lease to your EHR to the syringes in your exam drawer.

Chapter 8 opens with your physical location, lease contracts, and legal compliance. Whether you're leasing a suite, converting a room at home, or testing a hybrid model, there are zoning laws, ADA rules, and lease clauses you must understand before signing anything. We cover how to avoid hidden costs, negotiate improvements, and make sure your space aligns with your clinical and financial goals.

Chapter 9 focuses on your tech tools. Your electronic health record (EHR) system, scheduling tools, billing workflows, and HIPAA compliance all live here. We walk through popular EHRs, outline what to look for (and what to watch out for), and share practical advice on secure telehealth, e-faxing, and integrated billing systems, especially for those just starting out.

Chapter 10 is all about supplies and equipment. You'll learn how to set up Amazon Business, McKesson, and Henry Schein accounts, where to shop for secondhand medical equipment (yes, eBay is legit), and how to keep vaccine costs manageable by enrolling in programs like VFC and your state's immunization registry. We also include a section on choosing a reliable laser printer, because when your entire day depends on printing referrals and lab orders quickly, that $600 machine can become your best investment.

Chapter 11 walks through creating policies and protocols that protect your license, streamline your operations, and prepare you for audits. You'll learn how to build SOPs for labs, referrals, and emergencies, how to train new staff, and why a simple non-compete clause can protect your patient panel. These behind-the-scenes systems aren't flashy, but they are the backbone of a safe, scalable practice.

Chapter 12 guides you through hiring and leading your first team. We help you decide whether to bring on an MA, RN, or just front-office help, and explain how state scope-of-practice laws affect delegation, because not everything can be handed off legally. You'll also get advice on onboarding, retention, setting up payroll, and building a workplace culture that people want to stay in.

You don't need to do everything at once, though every decision in this section will shape how your practice feels to patients and how sustainable it is for you. This is the infrastructure that supports your care, protects your license, and keeps you sane. Let's build it right.

Chapter 8: Location, Lease, and Legal Landmines

Finding the right location for your practice is more than a matter of convenience; it's a strategic decision that affects your growth, accessibility, and compliance. Whether you're considering a brick-and-mortar space, working from a home office, or operating a hybrid model, there are zoning rules, lease clauses, and regulatory requirements you'll need to navigate. The right space can elevate your brand and support your clinical goals. The wrong one can cost you time, money, and credibility.

This chapter walks through what to consider when choosing your physical space, how to negotiate your lease, what legal pitfalls to avoid, and the hidden costs no one tells you about that you'll want to plan for.

Brick-and-Mortar vs. Home Office vs. Hybrid (and Mobile)

A standalone office offers visibility, patient trust, and room for growth, but it comes with overhead costs, lease agreements, and maintenance. A home office or virtual-only model offers flexibility and lower costs but may limit services and require stricter HIPAA compliance procedures. Hybrid models, where providers work from a home base part-time and rent space as needed (such as in a co-working medical facility), are growing in popularity. Mobile clinics are another creative option, especially for providers focused on underserved or rural populations. They offer maximum flexibility and community reach but require thoughtful planning around vehicle setup, licensing, and maintenance. Whatever you choose, your decision should reflect your patient population, your services, and your long-term vision.

> *Pro Tip:* Don't overlook parking. Many patients choose a provider based solely on how easily they can park. If your building has limited or distant parking, it could negatively impact retention, especially for elderly, disabled, or anxious patients. Remember, if you're

walking a quarter mile from your car each day, your patients will be too.

Lease Negotiations and Legal Oversight

If you go the brick-and-mortar route, your lease is one of your most important contracts. Don't rush it. Lease terms can either empower your growth or restrict your options. Negotiate lease length, renewal terms, exit clauses, and responsibilities for maintenance or repairs. Some landlords will agree to tenant improvement allowances (TIAs) to help fund your build-out. Others might include utilities, cleaning, or signage in the lease.

Always work with a healthcare-savvy real estate attorney before signing. There may be clauses related to medical waste disposal, subletting, Americans with Disabilities Act (ADA) compliance, or restrictions on certain types of services (such as, aesthetics or medication-assisted treatment) that can affect your operations.

Zoning, ADA, and Local Permits

Before signing a lease, check zoning regulations through your city or county planning department. Not all commercial spaces allow for medical use, even if the location looks ideal. You'll need confirmation that the space is zoned appropriately and that you can make any renovations you envision. Your space must also meet ADA standards. This includes entry ramps, parking, restrooms, and hallway widths. Non-compliance can lead to lawsuits or failed inspections. Also, ask your landlord if the building already has a Certificate of Occupancy (CO) for medical use. If not, you may need to apply, and that can delay your opening.

Hidden Costs to Watch Out For

Beyond rent, there are costs that can sneak up on you. These might include:

- CAM (Common Area Maintenance) fees in multi-tenant buildings
- Liability or property insurance beyond what's listed in your lease
- Required upgrades to plumbing or electrical systems for medical equipment
- Medical waste disposal contracts
- Biohazard signage or security features (especially for controlled substances)

- HIPAA-compliant shredding or secure storage
- IT setup and network security

Build a cushion in your startup budget for these surprises, and ask other local NPs or medical tenants in the building what they wish they'd known before moving in.

Final Thoughts

Your location sets the tone for your practice. It affects who finds you, how they experience your care, and whether your space grows with your goals. Whether you're leasing a suite or converting a spare room at home, the process requires foresight, flexibility, and legal protection. Next, we'll delve into the technology that supports modern NP practices, from selecting the right EHR to establishing a HIPAA-compliant digital infrastructure.

Chapter 9: EHRs, Tech, and Practice Management

Choosing the right technology for your practice isn't just about convenience; it's about efficiency, patient safety, and long-term success. From scheduling and charting to billing and compliance, the systems you choose will either streamline your day or create ongoing headaches. This chapter helps you evaluate, select, and integrate your core digital tools: your EHR (electronic health record), scheduling and telehealth platforms, billing software, and the cybersecurity tools you'll need to stay HIPAA-compliant in today's digital landscape.

Choosing Your EHR

Your EHR is the backbone of your practice. It affects how quickly you can chart, how easily you can e-prescribe, and how professionally you appear to patients and other providers. It should align with your specialty, workflow, and budget.

Popular options for NP-run practices include:

- **Athenahealth** : robust features, excellent billing support, higher cost.
- **CharmHealth**: affordable, customizable, good for integrative and wellness models.
- **Elation**: intuitive, strong focus on clinical workflow and continuity.
- **Jane**: well-suited for cash-pay or hybrid models with built-in scheduling.
- **SimplePractice**: popular with behavioral health, user-friendly for solo providers.

When evaluating, consider: Do you need built-in billing, or do you outsource? Will you offer telehealth? Do you need customizable templates? Also, be aware that many EHRs charge extra for essential features like integrated lab ordering, e-prescribing, and electronic faxing, so be sure to ask about pricing beyond the base subscription. Additionally, some EHR systems that include billing functionality charge a percentage of the collected revenue rather than a flat monthly subscription for charting. These systems can be especially appealing when you're starting out, since you only pay when you get paid, helping you manage cash flow. In contrast, other EHR platforms may charge separately for the charting system itself, while allowing you to outsource billing at a lower flat rate.

Personally, I use AthenaOne because it has integrated billing, is extremely user-friendly, has scheduling, integrated telehealth, and the only cost is a percentage of collections, meaning the company is motivated to support timely documentation and claims follow-through. This model helps reduce denials and billing delays. However, it's important to note that as your practice grows, this percentage-based model can become more expensive compared to flat-rate alternatives. Weigh these options carefully, considering your practice's size, revenue cycle management skills, and patient volume expectations. Request demos and test-drive the top two or three options before making a commitment. Also, ask what's included (fax integration? lab ordering?) and what costs extra.

Choosing a Telehealth Platform

Telehealth is now a core component of modern private practice. Choosing the right platform depends on your specialty, practice size, integration needs, and budget. Below is a comparison of popular standalone telehealth platforms and those integrated into EHRs.

What Is Telehealth and Why It Matters

Telehealth refers to the delivery of healthcare services remotely via telecommunications technology, most commonly through video visits. Even if your practice is primarily in-person, telehealth can be an invaluable tool. If a patient calls to cancel at the last minute due to transportation issues or a minor illness, you can quickly convert the appointment to a telehealth visit and still provide care while keeping your schedule intact. This flexibility helps reduce no-shows and supports continuity of care.

Telehealth also expands your reach to patients in rural or underserved areas who might not otherwise have access to your services. For providers in behavioral health, primary care, and chronic disease management, this flexibility can greatly improve accessibility, patient satisfaction, and revenue stability. For telehealth, make sure the platform is HIPAA-compliant and easy for patients to use. Many EHRs now include telehealth integration, although, alternatives like Doxy.me, Zoom for Healthcare, or Spruce can also work well, especially for solo or hybrid providers.

Standalone Telehealth Platforms

Platform	Features	Cost Structure	Notes
Zoom for Healthcare	High-quality video, screen sharing, waiting rooms	Subscription-based	Widely used but may require EHR linking
Doxy.me	Browser-based, no download, virtual waiting room, group calls	Free basic, paid professional tier	Great for small practices
VSee	Telemedicine-focused features, file sharing, screen share	Tiered pricing	Offers white-label options
Updox	Secure messaging, video, appointment reminders	Subscription	Works well for practices scaling up
Spruce Health	Secure communication, video visits, fax, SMS	Subscription-based	Excellent for mobile-first practices

EHRs with Integrated Telehealth

Many modern EHRs now include telehealth built directly into their system, streamlining documentation, billing, and patient communication.

EHR Platform	Integrated Telehealth?	Notes
SimplePractice	Yes	Excellent for behavioral health, seamless integration
Athenahealth	Yes	Enterprise-level EHR, strong analytics and billing
Kareo	Yes	Great for small-to-medium medical practices
Charm EHR	Yes	Customizable, patient portal with video visit support
Practice Fusion	Limited (via integrations)	Needs third-party plugin for full telehealth support

Comparing AI Scribe Services

AI medical scribes are revolutionizing how providers document encounters by reducing time spent on charting and improving workflow efficiency. These AI tools listen in on patient encounters (with patient consent) and draft clinical notes in real time, often suggesting codes and summarizing medical conversations in formats that match your EHR.

This can be especially helpful for solo or small practices where time is limited. Many systems even offer coding suggestions, SOAP formatting, and integration with billing tools. Some allow hands-free operation so you can remain fully present with the patient.

Below is a breakdown of the leading AI scribe solutions:

Scribe Platform	Features	EHR Integration	Cost	Notes
Suki	Ambient documentation, command-based charting	Epic, Cerner, Athena	Subscription	High accuracy, growing EHR compatibility
Nuance DAX	Uses Dragon AI, ambient listening, note generation	Deep Epic integration	Enterprise	Ideal for large systems, very accurate voice capture
Tali AI	Note drafting, real-time suggestions, coding help	FHIR-enabled EHRs	Affordable	Integrates with most major EHRs
Notable Health	Voice-activated notes, task automation	Epic, Cerner	Custom quote	More popular in enterprise settings
Scribe AI	Real-time note transcription, customizable templates	EHR-agnostic	Pay-per-use	Great for small to medium practices; flexible pricing

These tools vary in price and sophistication. If you're in a solo or small group setting, something like Suki or Scribe AI may be the most cost-effective, while larger clinics may benefit from Nuance DAX or Notable's enterprise-level features.

Pro Tip: Consider workflow efficiency, HIPAA compliance, EHR integration, and your specialty needs when choosing both telehealth and AI scribe platforms.

Scheduling and Billing Systems

If your EHR doesn't include scheduling or you need more robust features, consider stand-alone scheduling platforms that allow for online booking, automated reminders, and appointment confirmations.

Billing systems can be internal (through your EHR), outsourced to a billing service, or managed via third-party tools. Consider your payer mix; Medicaid and Medicare require precise claims handling, and determine whether you'll need assistance with prior authorizations, denials, or patient statements. If billing is not your strength, don't hesitate to hire a pro or contract with a trusted company.

HIPAA Compliance in a Digital World

Cybersecurity is not optional. HIPAA violations, even unintentional ones, can lead to serious fines and patient distrust. You are responsible for securing protected health information (PHI), whether it's stored digitally or discussed over a video visit.

Key elements of digital HIPAA compliance include:
- Encrypted email and messaging
- Secure cloud storage with audit logs
- Role-based access for staff
- Regular software updates and patches
- A Business Associate Agreement (BAA) with every tech vendor
- Secure faxing or e-fax options (such as, Updox, RingRx, or built-in through your EHR)

You'll also need written policies outlining how PHI is accessed, stored, and transmitted, and regular staff training if you're not working solo. Don't forget backups: ensure your systems auto-save data securely and frequently. If you're unsure about compliance, work with a healthcare IT consultant or use a HIPAA compliance toolkit from your malpractice carrier or professional organization.

Final Thoughts

The right tech stack is one of the most powerful assets in a modern NP practice. It reduces burnout, prevents errors, and enhances the patient experience. More than that, it frees up your time so you can focus on what matters most: providing excellent care. Next, we'll walk through policies and protocols that set the tone for safe, efficient, and patient-centered operations.

Chapter 10: Buying Equipment and Supplies

Outfitting your practice doesn't have to break the bank, but it does require a strategic approach, thorough research, and effective organization. From exam tables and otoscopes to syringes, vaccines, and IV fluids, you'll need to source equipment and supplies that are reliable, compliant, and affordable. This chapter guides you through setting up essential supply accounts, locating medical-grade equipment (both new and used), and approaches to vaccine purchasing. It also explains how to take advantage of discounts and federal assistance programs for pediatric immunizations.

Setting Up Supply Accounts

One of the easiest places to start is Amazon. With your NPI and business tax ID, you can create a free Amazon Business account specifically for medical providers. This gives you access to wholesale pricing, quantity discounts, and tax-exempt status on eligible purchases. It's ideal for basic medical supplies, PPE, cleaning products, and office essentials.

For clinical and pharmaceutical-grade supplies, including IV fluids and medications, you'll want to open accounts with distributors like Henry Schein and McKesson. Both allow you to register using your professional credentials and typically require an NPI, state license, and DEA number for ordering controlled substances or prescription medications.

In practice, it's common to compare prices across all three, Amazon, Henry Schein, and McKesson, before placing an order. While McKesson often has the best pricing for medications and IV fluids, Henry Schein may be better for clinical tools and vaccines, and Amazon is unbeatable for non-regulated supplies.

Medical Equipment on a Budget

Large expenses like exam tables, scales, otoscopes, and autoclaves don't always need to be brand new. eBay is a great starting point, especially for gently used items. Many sellers on eBay also operate their own medical supply websites, and after browsing or purchasing there, you can often work directly with the vendor for future purchases. This approach can save thousands when compared to buying everything brand new.

Before purchasing used equipment, confirm that it meets current safety standards and compliance guidelines, especially if it involves diagnostics, sterilization, or refrigeration. For anything that stores or delivers vaccines, make sure it's VFC-compliant if you plan to participate in that program.

Buying the Right Printer

An often overlooked but essential investment is your office printer. While it might be tempting to buy a $200-$300 inkjet printer, these devices tend to wear out quickly and cost far more in the long run due to high ink replacement costs and slower performance. After going through multiple lower-cost printers in a two-year period, I finally invested in a high-quality laser printer for about $600. It has lasted for years, prints incredibly fast, and has been indispensable for lab orders, patient referrals, and equipment requests. Laser printers not only last longer but also use toner cartridges that produce more pages at a lower cost per print than traditional ink. Time is money in a clinical setting, and when you're printing frequently, the speed and reliability of a laser printer pays for itself many times over.

Vaccines: Ordering and Tracking

Vaccines are one of the most complex and expensive parts of stocking a primary care or pediatric practice. To begin, you'll need to register with your state's immunization information system (IIS), which is the registry that tracks administered vaccines and patient immunization histories.

Here are a few examples:

- **WebIZ**: Kansas, Nevada, and a few others
- **CAIR**: California
- **ImmTrac2**: Texas
- **NYSIIS**: New York
- **Florida SHOTS**: Florida

Each state has its own enrollment process, so search for your state's program and begin registration early; it may take weeks to complete.

Enrolling in the VFC Program

If you plan to see pediatric Medicaid patients and administer vaccines in-office, you'll want to enroll in the Vaccines for Children (VFC) program. This federal initiative provides free vaccines to children who are enrolled in Medicaid, uninsured, or underinsured. Enrollment is intensive but worthwhile. It includes required training, strict specifications for refrigerators and freezers, certified thermometers with continuous monitoring, and periodic site inspections. You'll be responsible for maintaining temperature logs and storage compliance.

The benefit: VFC provides the actual vaccine products at no cost, which is critical since Medicaid typically does not reimburse for the vaccine itself, only the administration fee, and even that is inconsistent across states. If you're not enrolled, Medicaid patients may need to be referred to local health departments or receive costly vaccines from your private stock.

Vaccine Share Programs

If you plan to offer vaccines to privately insured or self-pay patients, look into vaccine share programs. These programs offer bulk purchasing, discounts, and distribution services through national or regional partners.

There are dozens of options, and the best fit depends on your practice size, specialty, location, and patient population. The American Academy of Pediatrics provides a helpful list and breakdown of these programs, available here: https://www.aap.org/en/patient-care/immunizations/implementing-immunization-administration-in-your-practice/managing-costs-associated-with-vaccinating/

Take time to compare and consult with vendors to find the right match.

Final Thoughts

Stocking your practice takes more than just a shopping list; it takes foresight, compliance, and savvy purchasing. Whether you're sourcing your first otoscope or preparing to order VFC vaccines, the right setup can save you thousands and reduce logistical headaches down the road. Next, we'll look at creating the internal systems, policies, procedures, and workflows that keep your practice running smoothly and prepare you for growth.

Chapter 11: Policies, Protocols, and Compliance

Behind every well-run practice is a solid set of policies, protocols, and compliance systems. These aren't just bureaucratic necessities; they're what allow you to run a safe, efficient, and patient-centered operation. Whether you're working solo or managing a team, written procedures help ensure consistency, prepare you for inspections, and support staff onboarding and accountability.

This chapter will guide you through the essential standard operating procedures (SOPs) for intake, labs, referrals, and emergencies; how to create training manuals for your staff; and what you need to do to prepare for audits and licensure renewals.

SOPs: Standard Operating Procedures for Common Workflows

Begin by documenting the tasks you or your staff perform on a daily basis. Consider each process carefully and write out clear, step-by-step instructions. These should be easy to follow and understandable even to a new hire. Your intake procedures should explain how to verify identity, collect insurance information, and document medical histories. For labs, your workflow should describe how specimens are labeled, documented, and collected or delivered to couriers.

Referrals should have a defined process too, including who generates them, how they are tracked, and what documentation is shared with specialists. Emergency protocols are equally important and should outline how to respond to on-site medical issues, when to call 911, and how to document incidents afterward. Don't overlook infection control policies, incident reporting procedures, and documentation standards. These procedures are not only critical for staff efficiency and safety, but they also serve as the foundation of your compliance strategy.

Creating Staff Manuals and Training Tools

Even if you only have one or two employees, a detailed staff manual can help eliminate confusion and protect your business. It should clearly describe job duties and role expectations. Include your office hours, policies on time off, guidelines for professional appearance and behavior, and rules about confidentiality and social media use.

The manual should also serve as a how-to guide for practice operations. This might include instructions for using your phone system, EHR software, scheduling platforms, and other tools. You can make these sections more effective by also creating short video tutorials or checklists saved in a shared folder. Your staff should receive annual training on HIPAA compliance, CPR (if applicable), infection control, and emergency procedures. Keep documentation of all training sessions, including sign-in sheets and any certificates earned. These records are often required for audits or licensing inspections.

It's also wise to include a basic non-compete clause in your employee agreements. This isn't about restricting someone from leaving your practice and continuing their career elsewhere. Instead, it protects the time and investment you've made in building a patient panel. You don't want someone to join your practice, develop rapport with your patients using your infrastructure and resources, and then leave to start their own practice, taking your patients with them. A well-written non-solicitation or non-compete agreement clarifies that while employees are free to move on professionally, they may not actively recruit, or transfer patients seen under your business. This kind of policy is particularly important in smaller communities or when your practice has a narrow specialty or loyal following.

Just as important: include a structured disciplinary process. Have a clear outline in your manual for how performance or conduct concerns will be addressed. This should include a progressive process of verbal warnings, written write-ups, and final notices. Every disciplinary action, no matter how minor, should be documented and stored in the employee's personnel file.

> **Pro Tip:** If you ever have to terminate an employee, you must be able to show a documented trail of the events and decisions that led

to that outcome. Without it, you're vulnerable to unemployment insurance claims or wrongful termination disputes. Even if someone "seems like a good fit," protect yourself with documentation. It's not about being harsh; it's about being fair, consistent, and legally covered.

Preparing for Audits and Licensure Renewals

Audits may come from insurance payers, Medicaid, OSHA, or your state board. The best way to handle them is to stay ready year-round. Keep your policies and licenses up to date and accessible. Conduct internal reviews every few months to ensure that logs are complete, records are stored securely, and staff credentials are up to date.

Maintain organized documentation for all relevant items, including temperature logs for vaccine storage and HIPAA training records. Confirm that your equipment is calibrated regularly and that drills, such as fire or emergency response, are done and documented. Store billing and communication records in an encrypted system, and make sure your EHR logs are audit ready. Licensure renewals can sneak up on you, so mark important deadlines at least 90 days in advance. Stay current on your own state license, DEA registration, controlled substance permits, and business licenses. Track your CEUs in a centralized folder, whether physical or digital, to avoid scrambling when it's time to renew.

Final Thoughts

Well-developed policies and procedures are not about red tape; they are what bring structure and accountability to your work. A thoughtfully organized system helps everyone on your team understand expectations, avoid errors, and focus on excellent care. In the next chapter, I'll discuss how to hire the right support, onboard them effectively, and establish a team culture that aligns with your mission.

Chapter 12: Hiring and Leading a Small Team

Hiring your first staff member is a major milestone. Whether it's a front office coordinator, a medical assistant, or an RN, the right support allows you to focus more on patient care and less on administrative tasks. Simply put, hiring isn't just about filling roles; it's about building a team culture that supports your values, protects your reputation, and enhances patient experience. In this chapter, we'll explore how to choose between common clinical and administrative roles, how to onboard and retain staff effectively, and how to establish payroll, HR systems, and a workplace culture that makes people want to stay.

MA vs. RN vs. Front Office: Choosing the Right Roles

The first step is defining what support you actually need. A front office coordinator is typically your first hire if you're running a physical space. They handle phones, check-ins, scheduling, insurance verification, and general patient flow. A good front office hire sets the tone for your practice.

Medical assistants (MAs) are a popular choice for clinical support. They can room patients, take vitals, assist with procedures, prepare labs, administer injections (depending on your state's scope), and even handle basic documentation. MAs are cost-effective and highly versatile.

Registered nurses (RNs) receive more extensive clinical training, which is particularly beneficial in settings that involve triage, patient education, IV therapy, or complex care management. RNs cost more, but they can be worth it, depending on the services you need.

Start with what you need most and grow from there. It's also essential to understand what clinical tasks you can legally delegate in your state. In many states, nurse practitioners are not permitted to delegate invasive procedures, such as injections or IV insertions, to medical assistants. These tasks may only be delegated to registered nurses (RNs) or other licensed personnel. That said, the COVID-19 pandemic prompted rapid regulatory changes, and more states have begun allowing NPs to delegate invasive tasks to "trained professionals" under specific supervision protocols.

Because scope-of-practice laws and delegation rules vary widely and are still evolving, it's crucial to call your state board of nursing or board of medicine to get a clear, up-to-date understanding of what is allowed. Assuming you can delegate without checking could put your license at risk, even if a neighboring state has more flexible rules. You don't have to build your entire team at once. In fact, slow growth often leads to better hiring decisions.

> **Pro Tip:** If your state nursing board allows for you to delegate to "trained professionals" make sure you have it explicitly stated or recorded of what a "trained professional" is. Are they referring to MAs? CNAs? Or simply a staff member that you have trained and documented their training. Don't assume. Assumptions can cost you a mark on your license for improper delegation.

Onboarding and Retention

Once you've hired someone, it's important to have a structured onboarding process. Even if your team is small, your new hire needs time to learn your systems, understand expectations, and integrate into your workflow. Begin with a welcome packet or orientation folder that outlines the practice's mission, policies, and key contacts. Provide job-specific training and shadowing time, along with written SOPs (from Chapter 11) they can reference later.

Retention isn't about big bonuses or flashy perks, it's about respect, clarity, and consistency. Communicate often. Offer feedback early and regularly. Be open to suggestions, especially from experienced staff who see patient needs from a different angle. When possible, show flexibility. Recognize life outside of work. A team that feels seen and supported is more likely to stay loyal and bring their best.

Payroll, HR, and Culture Setting

Setting up payroll is simpler than it sounds. Most practices begin with a payroll service, such as Gusto, ADP, or QuickBooks Payroll. These systems help you handle withholdings, tax filings, and direct deposit. If you offer benefits, these services often help manage those, too. HR support can also be outsourced. You don't need an internal HR department to stay compliant. You'll need a W-4, an I-9, a job description, and an employee handbook for every staff member. Keep all documents organized in a secure, private location.

Culture isn't built overnight; it just starts with you. The way you speak to patients, the way you handle conflict, and the tone you use with staff all create the emotional tone of your workplace. Make it a space where people feel comfortable asking questions and sharing ideas. Recognize and celebrate small wins. When your MA calmly manages a difficult patient or your front desk saves the day with scheduling, acknowledge it. People remember how you make them feel, and that's what builds team loyalty.

> *Pro Tip:* You probably shouldn't throw stress balls at your staff, even if they deserve it, or are your sister (;-) Lisa), your aim may be better than you intend…

Final Thoughts

Hiring is one of the most powerful investments you can make in your practice. Your team represents your brand, extends your care, and helps you stay sane during the busiest weeks. Start with roles that match your immediate needs, build clear systems for onboarding and retention, and never underestimate the power of a supportive work culture. Up next, we'll walk through the financial side, billing, coding, and how to get paid efficiently.

Section IV: Operating and Growing

Now that your foundation is built, it's time to shift from startup mode to sustainable growth. Section Four delves into the real-world operations that keep your practice thriving: how you bill, how you attract new patients, how you retain them, and how you expand services without compromising your values in the process.

Chapter 13 breaks down the nuts and bolts of billing, coding, and getting paid. You'll learn how to credential properly, build a defensible fee schedule, use modifiers the right way, and why integrated billing can save you weeks of back-and-forth with insurance companies. We'll also discuss payment models, ranging from cash pay and PPOs to memberships and hybrid billing, and how to maintain a steady revenue stream even when your clinical plate is full.

Chapter 14 focuses on marketing, without the fluff. From claiming your Google Business profile to building a clean, trustworthy website and gathering patient reviews, we show you how to be findable, credible, and clear about what you offer. Whether you're DIYing your website or outsourcing it, you'll learn how to lead with your mission and make your brand about more than just your logo.

Chapter 15 centers on what happens after the first visit: patient experience and reputation. It covers the simple systems that build loyalty, retain patients, and keep reviews positive, even when they're not perfect. You'll learn how to create welcoming workflows, handle feedback with professionalism, and set up reminders, follow-ups, and patient onboarding that make people feel seen, not rushed.

Chapter 16 explores what's next, whether that's adding new services like IV hydration, ketamine, PFTs, and advanced care planning, or scaling to multiple locations or providers. We walk through how to choose revenue streams that fit your clinical style and how to grow without losing what made your practice special to begin with. You'll also find tips for hosting community events, building strategic partnerships, and deciding when (and how) to bring on more help.

This section is where the practice you built starts to evolve. With the right systems and strategies, your day-to-day becomes smoother, your income more predictable, and your work more joyful. Next, we'll focus on protecting all that progress and preparing for what comes next.

Chapter 13: Billing, Coding, and Getting Paid

Billing and coding can feel overwhelming at first, but they are the financial engine of your practice. Whether you plan to bill insurance, offer cash-pay services, or employ a hybrid model, your ability to consistently and efficiently collect revenue will determine the sustainability of your practice. In this chapter, we'll review credentialing tips, how to create and submit clean claims, how to handle superbills and modifiers, and how to structure your payment options, from cash to cards to memberships.

Credentialing Tips

Before you can bill insurance companies, you'll need to be credentialed with each one. This process can take several months, so it's best to start early. Ensure your CAQH profile is up to date and matches your NPI, state license, malpractice insurance, and business address precisely. Inconsistencies, even minor ones, are one of the biggest causes of delays.

Be proactive and thorough. Submit your applications to Medicare, Medicaid, and all major commercial payers you plan to accept. Follow up regularly. Maintain a spreadsheet that includes contact names, submission dates, and next steps. If you are billing under your own practice (rather than an umbrella group or supervising physician), ensure that you are listed as an independent practitioner and that your Tax ID and group NPI are properly tied to your pay-to and billing addresses.

Fee Schedules, Superbills, Modifiers, and Clean Claims

Before diving into billing logistics, you'll need to establish a fee schedule, your official list of charges for each CPT code and service. This schedule must remain consistent across all payers. Legally, you cannot list different prices for the same service depending on the insurance company. The amount you charge (your "stated rate") should be the same for every patient, regardless of whether they have Medicaid, Medicare, or commercial insurance.

Here's where the distinction matters: Insurances don't pay you based on what you charge; they pay based on your contracted rate. Each insurance company has its own allowable rate, and once you're credentialed with them, they'll adjust your charge down to that contracted amount. For example, you may charge $150 for a service, but if your contract with Insurance A allows $95 for that CPT code, you'll be paid $95, regardless of the original charge.

For commercial insurance plans, especially PPOs, you may still receive a portion of your billed rate even if you're out of network. Some plans will pay a percentage of your full charge, and in rare cases, they may pay your full billed amount.

This is why setting your initial fees thoughtfully is so important. Don't undervalue your services just to seem affordable. At the same time, be mindful of how your rates will be perceived. Patients often receive Explanation of Benefits (EOBs) that show what you charged versus what insurance paid. Charging $500 for a 99213 visit may be strategic from a billing standpoint, but to a patient unfamiliar with industry norms, it can seem astronomical. It's all about finding that sweet spot, charging enough to reflect your value and leave room for partial reimbursements, but not so high that it alienates or frustrates your patients.

For example, I based my own rates on the Medicare Physician Fee Schedule and doubled the reimbursement rates. I rarely collect that full amount, however, I've found that insurers generally reimburse me around 120% of the physician Medicare rate. This gives me a sustainable buffer and positions my practice competitively while preserving patient trust. To support this process, I've included a list of common CPT codes and what they entail in the appendices. This reference can help you build a solid, defensible fee schedule and give you a better understanding of what services you're billing for most frequently.

A superbill is a document you provide to cash-pay patients so they can request reimbursement from their insurance. It lists diagnosis codes, procedure codes (CPTs), your NPI, your Tax ID, the date of service, and what was paid. Having a superbill template saved in your EHR or scheduling software makes this quick and easy. When billing insurance directly, your goal is to submit clean claims, accurate, complete, and on time. Errors in coding, missing information, or incorrect patient data can result in denials or payment delays.

This is where having integrated billing within your EHR becomes especially valuable, particularly when you're just starting out. Many insurance companies now require documentation, such as the full note, (which includes HPI, ROS, PE, A/P, and their social, family, and medical histories) for any claim billed above a 99213. With an integrated system, the billing software can flag these requirements before submission. For example, it can alert you if a note is missing, if a required NDC number for a medication isn't included, or if you've included two ICD-10 codes that a specific payer doesn't accept together. Instead of waiting weeks for a claim to be processed, rejected, and returned, the system proactively identifies and corrects these issues in real-time. That means fewer denials, fewer delays, and more claims paid the first time around.

To improve success, make sure your team (or billing company) understands which CPT codes match your services and which modifiers are needed for specifics like telehealth, prolonged services, or multiple procedures. Track claim submissions and rejections weekly. Identify patterns early so you can fix systemic issues before they affect cash flow. If you're new to billing, consider working with an experienced medical biller or service, even on a part-time basis.

Payment Options: Cash, Cards, Insurance, and Memberships

Offering multiple payment options makes your services more accessible and your billing more consistent. If you're insurance-based, have a clear payment policy for copays and deductibles. Use a HIPAA-compliant payment processor like Square for Healthcare, Stripe, or a billing integration within your EHR.

For cash-pay visits, be transparent about pricing and offer digital receipts. Many patients are willing to pay out of pocket for accessible, high-quality care, especially for services such as mental health, wellness, or niche specialties.

Membership models are another option, especially for direct primary care (DPC), wellness, or hormone clinics. Patients pay a monthly fee in exchange for a defined set of services. Just make sure your model is legally compliant in your state and that you have clear contracts and documentation. Also, consider offering prompt-pay discounts for self-pay patients who pay in full at the time of service. This can incentivize fast payment while remaining compliant with insurance rules.

Final Thoughts

Getting paid doesn't have to be a struggle, but it does require systems. Start with clean credentialing. Develop good billing hygiene. Offer patients flexibility in how they pay you. Whether you do it all in-house or hire help, don't let fear of coding or claims stop you from building a thriving, profitable practice. Next, we'll explore effective, affordable marketing strategies designed specifically for NPs.

Chapter 14: Marketing That Actually Works

Marketing doesn't have to mean expensive ads or flashy campaigns. In fact, the most effective marketing for nurse practitioner practices is often grassroots, local, and rooted in trust. People want to know who you are, what you do, and why you care. Your goal isn't just visibility; it's credibility. That starts with showing up online in a way that reflects your mission and speaks directly to the community you want to serve. This chapter will guide you through setting up your online presence, optimizing for search, leveraging patient reviews, and building a brand that is more than just a pretty logo.

Google My Business, SEO, Yelp, and Social Proof

The single most important thing you can do to get found online is to claim and optimize your Google Business Profile. This is what shows up when people search for terms like "NP near me" or "urgent care in [your town]." Ensure your profile includes accurate contact information, hours, website, services, and professional photos.

Encourage satisfied patients to leave Google reviews, ideally spaced over time, to boost your ranking and build credibility. Respond to reviews professionally and promptly, especially if someone leaves a less-than-perfect comment. Your response matters just as much as the review itself. If your patients use Yelp in your area, claim that profile too. It's not as powerful as Google for healthcare, but it still matters for reputation and SEO. Remember, SEO (search engine optimization) isn't just about keywords; it's about having a consistent name, address, phone number, and online presence across the web.

Website Must-Haves

Your website is your digital front door. It doesn't need to be fancy, but it must be functional, clear, and mobile-friendly. At a minimum, you should include a homepage that clearly states who you are and what you offer, an

"About" page with your credentials and personal story, a "Services" page that outlines what you treat and how to book, and contact info with a map, phone number, and secure contact form. Don't forget to include links to your patient portal, accepted insurance providers, or cash-pay pricing, as well as testimonials or reviews.

For building your site, several platforms now offer easy, intuitive tools to create a professional-looking website, even if you have zero design experience. Wix, Squarespace, and Weebly are popular drag-and-drop website builders with pre-designed healthcare templates and built-in hosting. They also offer logo creation tools and branding packages that allow you to choose from color palettes, fonts, and imagery that align with your mission.

GoDaddy Website Builder is another option that includes tools for scheduling, online payments, and mobile optimization. WordPress.com offers greater customization and plug-in support but may require a bit more tech-savviness or help from a freelancer.

If you'd rather not build it yourself, most of these platforms offer professional design services for a flat fee. You can also hire someone on Fiverr or Upwork to design and build your site and logo based on your vision and needs. Regardless of who builds it, focus on clarity, ease of navigation, and messaging that speaks to your patients' priorities.

Use a professional headshot, clean layout, and plain language. Avoid medical jargon. Speak like you would in a conversation with a patient.

Branding Your Mission (Not Just Your Logo)

Your brand isn't just your color palette or logo design; it's the feeling people get when they interact with your practice. Your mission should come through in everything you publish, say, or design.

Do you specialize in trauma-informed care? Family-centered medicine? LGBTQ+ wellness? Make that clear. Consistency across your social media, website, intake forms, and signage helps patients understand not just what you do, but why you do it.

Don't be afraid to share your story. Patients connect with authenticity. Tell them why you became a nurse practitioner. Share your values and vision for care. People are far more likely to refer their friends and family to a provider they trust.

If you're on social media, post content that aligns with your mission. Tips, personal messages, patient education, and behind-the-scenes content go a long way. You don't need to go viral, you just need to show up.

Final Thoughts

Marketing is less about selling and more about telling a story. If you can clearly communicate who you are, what you do, and why it matters, your ideal patients will find you. Up next, we'll dive into patient experience and reputation, and how to keep the people you've worked so hard to bring through the door.

Chapter 15: Patient Experience and Reputation Management

Bringing patients through the door is only half the battle, keeping them, and making sure they want to refer others, is where your long-term success lives. Reputation isn't something you can buy; it's something you build through every patient interaction, both in person and online. From the moment someone finds your website to the way you follow up after a visit, every step is a chance to either gain or lose trust. This chapter covers how to build loyalty through service, how to navigate negative reviews with professionalism and grace, and how to create systems that encourage patients to return and recommend you to others.

Building Loyalty Through Service

Patient loyalty begins with the small things: running on time, returning calls, and treating people with respect. Your front desk is your first impression, and your follow-up is your last. Make both count. Patients should feel seen, heard, and valued, especially during the intake and visit process. Invest in empathetic listening, nonjudgmental care, and efficient workflows. When a patient leaves feeling cared for and not rushed, they'll tell their friends. Simple touches matter, such as welcoming signage, comfortable waiting spaces, paperless forms, or even sending a thank-you text after a new patient visit. These moments are often more memorable than the clinical care itself.

Addressing Negative Reviews

No matter how skilled or compassionate you are, you will eventually receive a negative review. What matters most is how you respond. Never respond defensively or disclose any protected health information (PHI). A calm, professional reply that acknowledges the experience and invites follow-up offline shows maturity and concern.

For example: "Thank you for your feedback. We're sorry to hear your experience didn't meet expectations. We take concerns seriously and would welcome the chance to speak directly and make things right. Please reach out to us at [practice phone/email]." Use critical feedback as a lens. Was there a communication gap? A system issue? An unreasonable expectation? Not every criticism is valid, but every one is an opportunity to reassess your patient experience.

Creating Systems for Retention

You don't have to reinvent the wheel for every patient interaction. Build systems that consistently promote satisfaction, follow-up, and long-term retention. Automate appointment reminders via text or email. Use check-in surveys to catch dissatisfaction before it spills into a public review. Create follow-up workflows for labs, referrals, and chronic care patients so nothing falls through the cracks.

Consider developing a patient onboarding process that includes a welcome email, portal instructions, and information about your services. This creates clarity and connection from the start. Think about continuity, how are patients reminded of their next visit, annual check-up, or refill appointment? The easier you make it to return, the more likely they are to do so.

Final Thoughts

Exceptional care builds loyalty, but intentional systems keep it. Prioritize kindness, clarity, and communication in every interaction. Your reputation will grow not because you asked for it, but because you earned it. Next, we'll explore how to expand your services, grow with purpose, and discover new revenue streams that align with your mission.

Chapter 16: Beyond the Basics: Growing with Purpose

Once your foundation is strong, the question becomes: where do you go from here? Growth can take many forms, offering new services, reaching new communities, or building a team to help support demand. The key is purposeful growth that aligns with your values, your patient base, and your long-term vision. This chapter guides you through expanding your offerings, hosting community events, and scaling your team or physical footprint without compromising the mission that made your practice special in the first place.

Adding New Services

Adding services can both deepen your value to patients and open new revenue streams. You don't need to offer everything at once; start with the services that fit your training, interests, and community needs. IV hydration, vitamin injections, and wellness consults are low-barrier options that many patients request. If you're certified, ketamine therapy and TMS (transcranial magnetic stimulation) are growing in demand, especially in mental health practices.

Aesthetics like Botox, fillers, and microneedling can bring in cash-pay clients, while allergy testing and immunotherapy can be added with a bit of training and infrastructure. Joint injections are a great addition for primary care, ortho, and pain clinics. Consider what makes sense for your population.

Don't forget certifications like CDL medical exams; these are high-volume, relatively low-risk visits with strong referral potential. Group offerings (such as diabetes education, weight loss support, or trauma-informed care groups) not only bring in revenue but also build community engagement and trust. Another highly valuable service is chronic care management (CCM), especially for patients with ongoing physical or mental health conditions. CCM programs enable you to bill monthly for time spent coordinating care outside of face-to-face visits, such as phone check-ins, medication management, and referrals to therapy or specialty care. When paired with behavioral health integration, this approach can deliver both improved patient outcomes and predictable revenue for your practice.

Two more often overlooked but billable services are pulmonary function testing (PFT)/spirometry and advanced care planning (ACP). PFTs are valuable for diagnosing and managing asthma, COPD, and other chronic respiratory issues, and can be performed in-office with relatively low overhead. Advanced care planning, especially in older adult populations, is not only clinically meaningful, but it's also a separately billable visit when documented correctly. Adding these services increases your value to patients while strengthening the financial stability of your practice.

Hosting Community Events or Workshops

Becoming a visible, helpful presence in your community can boost both awareness and goodwill. Consider hosting blood pressure screenings, wellness fairs, or seasonal vaccination clinics. Partner with local gyms, yoga studios, or parent groups to offer health talks or Q&A sessions.

Workshops, whether in-person or virtual, on topics like stress management, hormone health, or nutrition, are low-cost ways to showcase your knowledge and engage new patients. Bring brochures, offer discounted consults, and capture emails for future marketing. These events help position you as a trusted community expert, which is marketing gold.

Expanding to Additional Providers or Sites

If you're consistently booked out, it might be time to grow your team. Bringing on another NP (or RN or MA) can help you extend hours, expand services, or serve more patients without burning out. Look for providers whose philosophy and communication style match yours.

Hiring support staff, such as a second front desk coordinator or a billing assistant, can also improve efficiency and patient satisfaction. Don't wait until you're overwhelmed; build capacity ahead of the curve. For those looking to open a second location, start by identifying your most loyal patient base. Would they travel? Is there an underserved area nearby with similar needs? Consider starting with a part-time satellite clinic before fully expanding.

Final Thoughts

Growth should be intentional, not impulsive. Focus on what patients are asking for, what aligns with your expertise, and what energizes you. Scaling with purpose ensures you stay fulfilled, sustainable, and grounded in your mission. Next, we'll look at how to protect that growth through smart risk management, self-care, and preparation for the future.

Section V: Protecting, Scaling, and Transitioning

By now, you've built the bones of your private practice, your systems are running, patients are coming through the door, and your mission is taking root in your community. Sustaining your practice in the long term requires more than just good intentions. It requires protection. It requires boundaries and a plan for the future.

Chapter 17 focuses on risk management, the not-so-glamorous but absolutely essential work of protecting your license, your livelihood, and your peace of mind. I'll cover how to choose the right malpractice insurance, what kind of legal support to have on standby, how to document defensively (without drowning in notes), and how to proactively set up protocols that reduce liability and increase clarity in your day-to-day.

Chapter 18 delves into the realities of scaling your practice without sacrificing the mission or joy that brought you here. Whether you're adding virtual assistants, hiring a team, or just trying to protect your evenings from being eaten by charting, this chapter walks you through how to delegate smartly, protect your work-life balance, and avoid burnout. Growth doesn't have to mean chaos; it can mean freedom, but only if you scale with intention.

Chapter 19 closes the loop by looking forward: exiting, selling, or transitioning your practice. You may not be ready to walk away today, but every thriving business should be built with the end in mind. Whether you envision selling to a larger group, bringing on a partner, or creating a legacy plan that passes your practice down to someone you trust, this chapter outlines how to plan so you can one day step back, gracefully, and with pride.

Chapter 17: Risk Management and Liability

No matter how experienced or careful you are, practicing medicine comes with risk. From clinical decisions to office protocols, documentation to communication, risk management is about identifying vulnerabilities before they become liabilities. The goal isn't to practice out of fear; it's to practice with clarity and confidence. This chapter covers malpractice insurance, charting best practices, when to consult a lawyer, and the defensive documentation habits that protect both your patients and your license.

Malpractice Insurance and Legal Protection

Even if you're not required to carry malpractice insurance in your state, you absolutely should. A single allegation, true or not, can cost tens of thousands of dollars in legal fees and damage your professional reputation. Select a policy with at least $1 million/$3 million in coverage, ensuring it aligns with your scope of services.

Decide between claims-made vs. occurrence coverage. Claims-made policies are cheaper upfront but require tail coverage if you switch or close your practice. Occurrence policies cover any claim made for services rendered during the policy period, regardless of when the claim is filed. Also consider general liability insurance (for slips, trips, or non-clinical risks), cyber liability (especially if you store patient info electronically), and business owner's policies that combine coverage types under one premium.

Charting Best Practices

Your documentation is your defense. It should be accurate, timely, and complete, but it doesn't need to be a novel. Focus on documenting what was said, what was done, and why.

Use objective language. Avoid judgmental phrasing like "non-compliant", instead, describe what occurred factually: "Patient reports missing doses of medication this week." Never chart in advance. Never copy/paste without reviewing for accuracy; and never alter a chart after the fact without properly documenting an amendment or late entry. If it's not documented, it didn't happen. This matters especially in the event of a claim or board review. Keep your charting concise but defensible.

When to Consult a Lawyer

Having a healthcare attorney in your corner isn't just for emergencies. Consult one when:

- You're forming your business or negotiating a lease
- You receive a subpoena or legal notice
- A patient files a complaint with the board
- You're facing a billing audit

An attorney can also review contracts, assist with staff employment agreements, or help you build a compliance plan. Investing in legal advice early can prevent costly problems later.

Defensive Documentation and Communication

Risk isn't always clinical. Misunderstandings, poor communication, or administrative gaps can also lead to conflict or complaints. When discussing care plans, especially ones with risks or alternatives, document the conversation in detail. Shared decision-making notes can go a long way in showing that the patient was informed. Set clear expectations, whether it's for controlled substance refills, test follow-ups, or missed appointment policies, and reinforce them in writing. If something goes wrong, document your actions and communication thoroughly. A well-documented, transparent response is often your best protection.

Final Thoughts

You can't eliminate risk entirely, but you can minimize it with thoughtful systems, good documentation, and proactive planning. The more you prepare ahead of time, the freer you are to focus on care. In our final chapter, we'll explore how to sustain your growth and protect your peace through smart delegation, self-care, and building your legacy.

Chapter 18: Scaling Without Losing Your Soul

Scaling your practice can be incredibly rewarding; however, it also comes with new pressures. As you take on more patients, more staff, and more responsibility, it's easy to lose the freedom and fulfillment that led you to private practice in the first place. The solution isn't to stop growing, it's to grow with boundaries, systems, and intention. This chapter explores how to delegate wisely, maintain your work-life balance, and avoid the kind of burnout that can drain the joy out of your purpose.

Delegation and Virtual Assistants

You cannot, and should not, do it all yourself. As your practice grows, you'll need to offload tasks that don't require your clinical brainpower. This may include hiring a second front desk staff member, outsourcing billing, or engaging a virtual assistant (VA) to handle tasks such as email management, prior authorizations, referral coordination, and social media management.

Virtual assistants are a cost-effective way to maintain efficiency without overloading your on-site team. Many VAs are trained in medical admin and EHR workflows and can be contracted through agencies that specialize in healthcare support.

Learn to delegate by asking: "Is this the highest and best use of my time?" If not, it's likely a task that can be systematized or handed off. Delegation protects your energy for what only you can do: clinical decision-making, strategic planning, and nurturing your patient relationships.

> *Pro Tip:* Don't Ignore the "Knock and Lure." When your staff gently knocks on the door or finds a reason to pull you out of a room mid-conversation, trust them. They're not being rude; they're managing your schedule and protecting your time. Chatty patients can derail your entire day, and while building rapport is important, so is respecting the time of every patient who follows. Teach your team to

be your timekeepers, and then actually listen when they step in to save you.

Work-Life Balance as a Business Owner

Owning a business doesn't mean being available 24/7. If anything, protecting your boundaries becomes more important as your practice scales. Set specific work hours and honor them. Don't check your EHR after dinner unless it's an emergency. Don't respond to patient messages on weekends. If you don't set these boundaries, no one else will. Build time into your week for deep work (writing notes, reviewing labs, planning growth, etc.) and time away from your screen entirely. Give yourself permission to rest, travel, or simply disconnect. The health of your business depends on your own health, too.

Avoiding Burnout

Burnout doesn't happen all at once; it builds gradually, through chronic overwork, unclear expectations, and unmet emotional needs. Preventing it starts with systems. Automate what you can. Delegate what drains you. Streamline your patient workflows to ensure your day isn't dictated by inefficiencies. Emotionally, you need connection. Whether it's a mentor, a peer group, or a therapist, have someone in your life who understands the unique stressors of being a clinician-entrepreneur, and remember your "why." Revisit your mission statement, your goals, and your impact. The more connected you are to your purpose, the easier it is to navigate the challenges.

> ***Pro Tip:*** Ask for Help. Your Staff Has Your Back. Don't wait until you're running on fumes to say something. Your front office team manages your schedule for a reason; they are your gatekeepers. If your days start feeling chaotic or unsustainable, speak up. Let them know you're hitting the burnout zone and need support protecting your time. A slight adjustment in how appointments are booked or scheduled can help restore your sanity. You don't have to do it all alone; lean on the systems and people you've put in place to support you.

Final Thoughts

Scaling doesn't mean sprinting. Grow at a pace that feels aligned with your values and your bandwidth. Protect your peace, your passion, your purpose, and your practice will flourish in ways that are truly sustainable. In our final section, I'll discuss what comes next: selling, transitioning, or creating a lasting legacy.

Chapter 19: Exiting, Selling, or Partnering Your Practice

Every practice has a life cycle, and whether you're thinking five years ahead or fifty, it's worth considering how you'll one day step back. Maybe you'll sell your practice, pass it on, or merge with a partner. Planning for that transition doesn't mean you're done; it means you're smart. This chapter explores how to build a practice with long-term value, what to consider when partnering or getting acquired, and how to leave a legacy that reflects your vision.

Building a Practice That's Sellable

Whether or not you plan to sell your practice, operating as if you will make your business stronger and more valuable. That means:

- Keeping clean financial records
- Running systems that don't rely on you alone
- Maintaining patient satisfaction and loyalty
- Documenting policies, procedures, and workflows

Buyers or partners want to invest in something sustainable. If your practice falls apart without you, it's not a business, it's a job. To build value, start detaching your identity from daily operations. Train others, delegate responsibilities, and keep clear records of performance metrics. You should also work with a CPA or business broker to assess the value of your practice, based on revenue, assets, contracts, and goodwill.

Partnership and Acquisition Options

Some NPs sell to larger healthcare groups or local hospital systems. Others merge with another NP-owned clinic to expand reach and reduce overhead. Both routes require clear contracts and aligned visions. Before entertaining offers, know your non-negotiables. Will you stay on for a transition period? Are you willing to relinquish your naming rights or switch to a new EMR? Do you want to retain ownership in part or exit fully?

If you're partnering, be sure to vet the other party's communication style, clinical philosophy, and long-term goals. Consider starting with a shared-services agreement or trial partnership before formalizing a legal merger. A healthcare attorney is essential throughout this process to protect your interests, clarify legal obligations, and avoid regrets.

Legacy Planning

Not every exit is about profit. Some NPs want to pass their practice to a colleague, child, or rising provider within the practice. Others want to create a nonprofit arm, scholarship fund, or community program. Think about what impact you want your practice to leave. What would make you proud? Your legacy might be a physical space, a clinical model, a mentorship program, or even just a reputation for compassionate, high-quality care. Whatever you envision, start planning early. Legacy doesn't happen by accident.

Final Thoughts

Exiting your practice isn't the end of your story; it's the beginning of a new chapter. Whether you sell, partner, or pass the torch, doing so with clarity ensures your years of work have a lasting impact. In our closing section, I'll offer final words of encouragement and tools to help you take the next step with confidence.

Conclusion: Owning It

Final Words of Encouragement

Starting, running, and scaling your own practice as a nurse practitioner is not just a business move; it's a deeply personal and courageous choice. You've chosen to carve your own path, to meet patients on your terms, and to create a practice that reflects your values. That takes grit, vision, and heart.

Along the way, you'll question yourself. You'll have late nights, tough patients, and unexpected bills, but you'll also have freedom, flexibility, and the joy of knowing your care makes a difference, on your terms. If you've made it this far in the book, you're already ahead of the curve. You've thought through the why, the how, and the what's next. You've invested in your own learning, which means you're not just dreaming, you're planning.

How to Know If You're Ready

No one ever feels 100% ready to open a practice. There will always be one more credential, one more savings goal, one more piece of advice to chase. Readiness isn't about having everything figured out; it's about having the willingness to start, the humility to learn, and the resilience to adapt.

If you:

- Know your "why" and feel called to do this
- Are prepared to work hard and grow into leadership
- Have a financial cushion, a working plan, and trusted support

…then you are ready enough. You can always refine your systems, expand your services, and tweak your strategy, but you can't build anything if you don't begin.

Resources and Next Steps

You don't have to do this alone. In the appendices, you'll find:

- ☐ A sample business plan

- ☐ A credentialing checklist

- ☐ A comparison table for EHRs and billing platforms

- ☐ A CPT code guide by specialty

- ☐ Resources for grants and startup help

- ☐ Private practice toolkit

- ☐ A fee schedule and payer rate worksheet

- ☐ Sample letter to insurance requesting reimbursement adjustment

Consider connecting with local NP business owners, joining a mastermind group or networking organization, and exploring national associations like the AANP or your state board for ongoing support. Finally, bookmark this book. You'll come back to it, chapter by chapter, as your practice grows. You've got this. Your future patients are lucky to have you.

Appendices

Sample Business Plan Templates

Below are two sample business plans inspired by real NP-led startup practices (with names and some details changed for confidentiality). These can be adapted to match your own practice vision.

Business Plan Example 1: Sunrise Wellness and Family Care

Owner: Jessica Lane, FNP-C

Location: Flagstaff, Arizona

Mission Statement: To deliver whole-person care to underserved families in northern Arizona by blending primary care with accessible wellness services.

Services:

- Family medicine
- Chronic care management
- Women's health
- Preventive wellness labs and IV hydration
- Telehealth for rural communities

Target Population: Low-income families, underinsured adults, and rural patients seeking accessible, high-quality care.

Revenue Model: Hybrid: accepting Medicaid, select commercial plans, and cash-pay.

Start-Up Costs:
- Office buildout (leased suite): $28,000
- EHR and telehealth platform: $2,000 startup + % collection model
- Lab contracts, licenses, insurance: $7,500
- Marketing and website: $3,500
- Total: ~$41,000

SWOT Highlights:
- Strength: Bilingual provider; limited local competition
- Weakness: Minimal admin staff at launch
- Opportunity: Expansion to mobile visits
- Threat: State Medicaid delays

Marketing Plan: Launched with Facebook community page, local radio spots, and an open house at launch.

Business Plan Example 2: Haven Mental Health & Recovery
Owner: Marcus Chen, PMHNP-BC
Location: Eugene, Oregon
Mission Statement: To restore mental health dignity through inclusive, evidence-based psychiatric care with a focus on trauma recovery and addiction support.
Services:
- Psychiatric evaluations and medication management
- MAT (Suboxone)
- Ketamine therapy
- Group therapy and wellness coaching
- Chronic pain and mood disorder support

Target Population: Adults with treatment-resistant depression, trauma survivors, and patients in opioid recovery.

Revenue Model: Primarily cash-pay; accepts limited out-of-network reimbursements and sliding scale for VFC patients.

Start-Up Costs:
- Space and furnishings: $18,000
- Legal and credentialing: $4,200
- Advanced malpractice (ketamine): $5,800
- EHR with billing module: $3,000
- Total: ~$31,000

SWOT Highlights:
- Strength: Niche market, strong word-of-mouth
- Weakness: Limited insurance credentialing
- Opportunity: Add TMS services and partner NP
- Threat: Local stigma around ketamine therapy

Marketing Plan: Instagram-based mental health advocacy; partnered with a yoga studio and trauma center for referrals.

Credentialing Checklist

- ☐ NPI (Type 1 and Type 2)
- ☐ State license, prescribing license and DEA
- ☐ Business license
- ☐ EIN/Tax ID
- ☐ CAQH profile (updated and attested)
- ☐ Malpractice insurance (with policy declaration page)
- ☐ Medicare and Medicaid enrollment (PECOS)
- ☐ Commercial insurance applications (payer portals)
- ☐ Signed W-9
- ☐ Copy of practice lease or proof of practice location

EHR Comparison Table

EHR System	Flat Fee Option	% of Collections	Integrated Billing	eRx & Lab Integration	Fax Support	Schedule Tools	Patient Portal	Support & Onboarding
AthenaOne	No	Yes	Yes	Yes	Yes	Yes	Yes	Strong
Charm	Yes	No	L	Yes	Yes	Yes	Yes	Mod
Elation	Yes	No	No	Yes	Yes	Yes	Yes	Mod
Kareo	Yes	No	Yes	Yes	L	Yes	Yes	Strong
SimplePractice	Yes	No	No	No	L	Yes	Yes	Basic
AdvancedMD	Yes	O	Yes	Yes	Yes	Yes	Yes	Strong

Limited = **L**
Optional = **O**

CPT Codes by Specialty and Modifiers

Primary Care/Common Codes:

- 99202–99205: New patient visits
- 99212–99215: Established patient visits
- 99406–99407: Smoking cessation
- 99495–99496: Transitional care mgmt.
- 99490: Chronic care management
- 99497: Advanced care planning
- 94760: PFT/spirometry
- 36415: Routine venipuncture
- G0444: Annual depression screening

Women's Health & OB:

- 88175: Pap smear, liquid-based cytology
- G0101: Pelvic and breast exam
- 81025: Urine pregnancy test
- 59425: OB antepartum care (4–6 visits)
- 11981: Insertion of non-biodegradable drug delivery implant

Psychiatry/Mental Health:

- 90791: Psych diagnostic evaluation
- 90833/90836: Psychotherapy add-on
- 99484: Behavioral health integration
- G2082: Spravato, 56mg–admin, monitoring, eval
- G2083: Spravato, 84mg–admin, monitoring, eval

Addiction Medicine:

- G0477–G0483: Drug screen testing
- H0001: Substance abuse assessment
- H2036: Residential treatment per diem

Procedural/Aesthetic:

- 20600: Small joint injection (finger, toe)
- 20605: Medium joint injection (wrist, ankle, elbow)
- 20610: Large joint injection (knee, shoulder, hip)
- 20552/20553: Trigger point injections
- 17000: Cryotherapy of benign lesions
- 17110: Cryotherapy of premalignant lesions (e.g., actinic keratosis)
- 11900: Injection, intralesional
- 96365: IV infusion (1st hour)

Annual Preventive Exam Codes:

- 99381–99387: Preventive visits (new patients, by age group)
- 99391–99397: Preventive visits (established patients, by age group)

Modifier Usage Notes:

Modifiers are essential tools for ensuring accurate reimbursement and avoiding denials, particularly when billing for multiple services on the same day. However, each payer has different rules, so it's important to double-check with their provider manuals.

- **Modifier 25** should be used when an E/M service is performed on the same day as a procedure (such as, a sick visit plus cryotherapy). It tells the payer that the E/M was separate and necessary beyond the pre-procedure work. However, many insurers will not pay for both a preventive exam and a problem-focused visit on the same day, even with a 25 modifier.

- **Modifier 59** is used to indicate procedures that are distinct or performed at different sites or times, such as a pap smear and cryotherapy. Still, many payers do not reimburse for both unless the documentation clearly supports the need for separate services.
- **Modifier 95 or GT** applies to telehealth visits depending on payer requirements. Medicare tends to use GT, while commercial payers often recognize 95. Documentation should include consent and that the visit was synchronous.
- **Modifier 24** is necessary when billing for an E/M service during a post-operative period that is unrelated to the surgery.
- **Modifier 57** is used to indicate that the E/M service led to a decision for surgery, which is often required for pre-operative visits scheduled within the global period.
- **Modifier 50**: Used to denote a bilateral procedure. If performing procedures such as bilateral joint injections or ear lavages, this lets payers know the procedure was done on both sides.
- **RT and LT**: Always use 'right' (RT) and 'left' (LT) when billing procedures like joint injections, nail removal, or skin tag removals to indicate side-specific services. Some payers will not reimburse without these distinctions.
- **Medication Billing Reminder**: When administering joint injections (CPT 20610), remember to also bill for the medications used, like corticosteroids (J3301 for triamcinolone). Failing to do so means you're essentially giving away the medication for free, which is pricey.

Additionally, some procedure codes, such as joint injections (20610), advanced dermatologic procedures, or higher-level mental health interventions, may require prior authorization depending on the payer. Even with the correct modifier, these may be denied if prior auth wasn't obtained. Always verify with each insurance company to see which combinations they will or won't reimburse. Using these modifiers incorrectly or inconsistently is one of the top reasons claims get rejected.

Resources for Grants and Startup Help

- **HRSA Nurse Corps Loan Repayment Program**: for NPs working in underserved areas.
- **National Health Service Corps (NHSC)**: loan repayment for clinicians in high-need communities.
- **Small Business Development Centers (SBDCs)**: free advising and training for entrepreneurs (https://americassbdc.org/).
- **SBA Microloans and 7(a) Loans**: federal funding programs to help with startup and operational costs (https://www.sba.gov/funding-programs/loans).
- **State Primary Care Offices (PCOs)**: offer state-level loan repayment or grant programs.
- **Hello Alice**: small business grants and support for underrepresented founders (https://helloalice.com).
- **GrantWatch**: searchable database for healthcare startup and nonprofit grants (https://grantwatch.com).
- **Nurse.org Grants & Resources Hub**: curated list of funding and tools for nurses in business (https://nurse.org/resources/).

These resources offer a solid starting point for funding, training, and networking as you build and grow your private practice.

Private Practice Toolkit

Your practice success is rooted not only in clinical expertise but also in having the right administrative and operational tools. Below are downloadable and customizable tools to help streamline operations from day one:

- **Sample Intake Packet**: including demographic forms, health history, consent to treat, HIPAA notice, and financial policy.
- **Superbill Template**: pre-filled with common CPT codes and modifiers, customizable by specialty.
- **Fee Schedule Worksheet**: editable spreadsheet to input and track charges across different payers.
- **Credentialing Tracker**: to keep progress organized across Medicaid, Medicare, CAQH, commercial plans, and PECOS.
- **New Hire Onboarding Checklist**: covers credentialing, immunization verification, training, and system logins.
- **Policy and Procedure Templates**: for common office operations (no-show policy, refill policy, referral workflows, etc.)
- **Patient Satisfaction Survey Template**: a printable or digital format to track service feedback.
- **Referral Directory Template**: customizable database for local specialists, imaging, labs, and behavioral health services.
- **Social Media & Marketing Calendar**: editable planner to map out health topics, events, and seasonal campaigns.

These tools can be printed and stored as a physical binder or imported into practice management software. Keeping these resources centralized will save you time and help maintain consistency as your practice grows.

https://drive.google.com/file/d/16e-fY1HbKNAJq1BSo0icPP3G6cMU-cJL/view?usp=drive_link

Sample Reimbursement Adjustment Letter

To Whom It May Concern:

I am writing to formally request a review and adjustment of the reimbursement rates associated with our provider contract. We are a nurse-practitioner-led healthcare practice offering (primary care, mental health, dermatologic, etc.) services and advanced procedures to a broad patient population. Our team includes experienced nurse practitioners trained in evidence-based approaches across the continuum of care.

We are also certified providers of advanced services such as (List all your services, mental health, dermatology, etc.). These services are performed by credentialed, board-certified practitioners with proper training and oversight. Our clinic remains committed to increasing access to comprehensive care within our community; however, reimbursement disparities among payers present a significant barrier.

We are requesting reimbursement updates on the following CPT codes, which reflect the scope of our services and align with the prevailing market rates in our region. These rates are based on a combination of the Medicare fee schedules, regional averages, and private payer benchmarks.

CPT Code	Description	Medicare Rate	Average Private Payer Rate	Requested Rate
99213	Established patient visit (15-29 min)	$X	$X	$X
99214	Established patient visit (30-39 min)	$X	$X	$X
99215	Established patient visit (40-54 min)	$X	$X	$X
99395	Preventive visit (age 18-39)	$X	$X	$X
G2082	Spravato Admin, 56mg	$X	$X	$X
G2083	Spravato Admin, 84mg	$X	$X	$X
20610	Major joint injection	$X	$X	$X
17000	Cryotherapy of benign lesion	$X	$X	$X
17110	Cryotherapy of premalignant lesion(s)	$X	$X	$X
99417	Prolonged E/M service (add-on)	$X	$X	$X

Our reimbursement from your organization currently falls below these benchmarks, limiting our ability to sustain the level of access and quality we strive to offer. Many private payers reimburse between 115%–120% of the current Medicare Physician Fee Schedule, and even state Medicaid programs have increased their rates since the passage of parity legislation.

We respectfully request that our contract be reviewed and adjusted accordingly to reflect the value of the care we provide, the regional standard for reimbursement, and the costs associated with maintaining comprehensive services. We are committed to continuing our partnership and ensuring that your members have access to care.

Thank you for your time and consideration.

Sincerely,

[Your Name], [Credentials]
[Practice Name]
[Address]
[Phone]
[Email]

Bibliography

American Academy of Nurse Practitioners. (n.d.). *AANP*. https://www.aanp.org

American Medical Association. (2023). *CPT Professional 2023*. AMA Publishing.

American Nurses Credentialing Center. (n.d.). *ANCC*. https://www.nursingworld.org/ancc

American Psychological Association. (2020). *Publication manual of the American Psychological Association* (7th ed.). American Psychological Association.

Athenahealth. (n.d.). *Athenahealth EHR*. https://www.athenahealth.com

Centers for Medicare & Medicaid Services. (n.d.). *CMS*. https://www.cms.gov

ChiroTouch. (n.d.). *ChiroTouch EHR*. https://www.chirotouch.com

Clockwise.MD. (n.d.). *Patient flow and wait time solutions*. https://www.clockwisemd.com

ClinicalTrials.gov. (n.d.). *A service of the U.S. National Library of Medicine*. https://www.clinicaltrials.gov

Current Procedural Terminology (CPT®). (n.d.). American Medical Association.

DrChrono. (n.d.). *EHR and practice management software*. https://www.drchrono.com

Doxy.me. (2023). *Telemedicine for everyone*. https://doxy.me

eClinicalWorks. (n.d.). *EHR solutions*. https://www.eclinicalworks.com

Electronic Fund Transfer (EFT) & Electronic Remittance Advice (ERA) Standards. (n.d.). Centers for Medicare & Medicaid Services. https://www.cms.gov

Front Office GURU. (n.d.). *Medical practice front desk training*. https://www.frontofficeguru.com

Health Insurance Portability and Accountability Act of 1996, 42 U.S.C. § 1320d et seq. (1996).

HealthIT.gov. (n.d.). *Telehealth and remote patient monitoring*. U.S. Department of Health and Human Services. https://www.healthit.gov

Henry Schein, Inc. (n.d.). *Medical, dental, and veterinary supplies & services*. Retrieved from https://www.henryschein.com

Insurance credentialing and payer enrollment requirements. (n.d.). Varies by state.

Kareo. (n.d.). *Kareo EHR*. https://www.kareo.com

McKesson. (2023). *Medical supplies and healthcare technology solutions*. https://www.mckesson.com

Medicaid State Programs. (n.d.). Varies by state (Medi-Cal, TennCare, MassHealth).

Medicare Provider Enrollment, Chain, and Ownership System. (n.d.). *PECOS*. https://pecos.cms.hhs.gov

ModMed. (n.d.). *Modernizing Medicine EHR*. https://www.modmed.com

National Council for Prescription Drug Programs. (n.d.). *NCPDP*. https://www.ncpdp.org

National Provider Identifier (NPI). (n.d.). National Plan and Provider Enumeration System.

Nevada Medicaid Provider Enrollment. (n.d.). https://www.medicaid.nv.gov

Nuance Communications. (2023). *Nuance DAX ambient clinical intelligence*. https://www.nuance.com/healthcare/ambient-clinical-intelligence.html

Office Ally. (n.d.). *Practice management and clearinghouse solutions*. https://www.officeally.com

Open Practice Solutions. (n.d.). *Medical billing and EHR*. https://www.openpracticesolutions.com

Optum Pay. (n.d.). *Provider payment solutions*. https://www.optumpay.com

PECOS Enrollment Guide. (n.d.). Centers for Medicare & Medicaid Services. https://pecos.cms.hhs.gov

Practice Fusion. (n.d.). *EHR for independent practices*. https://www.practicefusion.com

SimplePractice. (n.d.). *Practice management for health and wellness professionals*. https://www.simplepractice.com

Spruce Health. (n.d.). *All-in-one communication platform for healthcare.* https://www.sprucehealth.com

Suki AI. (2023). *Suki: The AI-powered voice assistant for doctors.* https://www.suki.ai

Tali AI. (2023). *Medical voice assistant for clinicians.* https://www.tali.ai

TherapyNotes. (n.d.). *Practice management software for behavioral health.* https://www.therapynotes.com

U.S. Department of Health and Human Services. (n.d.). *Understanding health insurance coverage.* https://www.hhs.gov

U.S. Small Business Administration. (n.d.). *SBA.* https://www.sba.gov

Updox. (n.d.). *Healthcare communication platform.* https://www.updox.com

Zoom Video Communications. (2023). *Zoom for Healthcare.* https://explore.zoom.us/en/healthcare

Acknowledgments

This journey would not have been possible without the unwavering support and encouragement of the people who walked beside me, especially during the most chaotic, uncertain early days.

To my sister, Lisa, thank you for dropping your entire life a state away to help me stabilize mine. After barely surviving my first year in private practice, overwhelmed by what I didn't know, you showed up with clarity, courage, and the kind of selfless dedication I can never repay. You helped lay the foundation, implementing policies, organizing workflows, and being the boots on the ground when I was still figuring out where to step. This would not have happened without you, and I will be forever grateful.

To my staff, thank you for growing with me, for figuring it out alongside me, and for sticking around through every insurance denial, policy rewrite, and stress ball thrown across the room. Your resilience and teamwork made this practice more than just a business; it became a mission.

To my patients, thank you for believing in me, for referring your friends and family, and for voting us "Best of Northern Nevada." Your trust, stories, and loyalty have been the heartbeat of this practice and the reason I keep going.

To my "two other husbands," Cameron and Andy, thank you for lighting the match that sparked this journey. Your encouragement and belief in me were the initial flame that turned into a wildfire of determination and vision. You saw something in me before I fully did, and your early support helped build the courage I needed to leap. You were the kindling that ignited a purpose bigger than all of us.

Thank you everyone. This book is as much yours as it is mine.

About the Author

Dr. Pauline Stoltzner, PhD, MSN, APRN, FNP-BC, PMHNP-BC, CSAP is a dual board-certified nurse practitioner in family and psychiatric medicine, founder of one of the most successful NP-owned practices in Northern Nevada, and a nationally recognized educator and advocate for advanced practice nursing. With a doctorate in education specializing in instructional design and educational technology, she has helped thousands of students, clinicians, and healthcare entrepreneurs learn how to translate clinical expertise into sustainable, patient-centered private practice.

After launching her own clinic while navigating the complexities of insurance billing, staffing, policy development, and credentialing, Dr. Stoltzner became passionate about empowering other nurse practitioners to confidently build practices of their own. Her firsthand experience, from policy hurdles to late-night EMR battles, brings authenticity and clarity to every chapter of this book.

In addition to her clinical work, Dr. Stoltzner teaches at the university level, serves as Director-at-Large for the Nevada Nurses Association, and was named one of Nevada's "50 Under 50" nursing leaders. She has published widely viewed instructional content on psychiatric assessment, adolescent substance use, and healthcare technology, and has been a presenter at nursing conferences across the western U.S.

She resides in Reno, Nevada, with her husband Roy and their two daughters, Lilly and Sophia, who continue to be the inspiration behind every big leap she takes. When she's not seeing patients or coaching aspiring practice owners, you'll find her cheering from the sidelines at gymnastics meets or designing educational tools to make healthcare more human and accessible.

www.ingramcontent.com/pod-product-compliance
Lightning Source LLC
Chambersburg PA
CBHW072241290326
41934CB00008BB/1370